ଔ

BECOMING HUMAN, BECOMING DIVINE

Becoming Human, Becoming Divine

The Christian Life According to
Blessed Columba Marmion

Columba McCann OSB

VERITAS

Published 2022 by
Veritas Publications
7–8 Lower Abbey Street
Dublin 1
Ireland
publications@veritas.ie
www.veritas.ie

ISBN 978 1 80097 044 1

10 9 8 7 6 5 4 3 2 1

A catalogue record for this book is available from the British Library.

Designed by Jeannie Swan, Veritas Publications
Printed in the Republic of Ireland by SPRINT-print Ltd, Dublin

Veritas Publications is a member of Publishing Ireland.

Veritas books are printed on paper made from the wood pulp of managed forests.
For every tree felled, at least one tree is planted, thereby renewing natural resources.

For the Redemptoristines at St Alphonsus Monastery, Drumcondra, where Blessed Columba was chaplain many years ago.

Contents

Acknowledgements

The idea of writing this book to mark the centenary of the death of Blessed Columba Marmion came from monks and oblates of Glenstal Abbey, and I am very grateful for their encouragement. Thanks to Br Emmaus O'Herlihy OSB, whose graphic art work formed the basis for the front cover design of the book. Thanks also to all the team at Veritas Publications, in particular Síne Quinn and Greg Daly, whose editorial work had a very significant impact on both the style of the book and its final text.

Abbreviations

Writings of Blessed Columba Marmion

CIHM   Blessed Columba Marmion, *Christ In His Mysteries*
(1919), reproduced in Dom Columba Marmion,
OSB, *Spiritual Writings*, P. Lethielleux (ed.) (Paris:
Buchet/Chastel, Pierre Zech Éditeur, 1998).

CLS   Blessed Columba Marmion, *Christ, The Life of the
Soul* (1918), reproduced in Dom Columba
Marmion, OSB, *Spiritual Writings*, P. Lethielleux (ed.)
(Paris: Buchet/Chastel, Pierre Zech Éditeur, 1998).

SW   Dom Columba Marmion, OSB, *Spiritual Writings*,
P. Lethielleux (ed.) (Paris: Buchet/Chastel, Pierre
Zech Éditeur, 1998).

Other sources

CCC   *Catechism of the Catholic Church*

GIRM   *General Instruction of the Roman Missal*

Introduction

The influence of Blessed Columba Marmion on Catholic spirituality in the twentieth century was immense. This Dublin-born spiritual teacher was not a reformer, but the strong liturgical and scriptural features of his personal spirituality anticipated important aspects of the renewal promoted by the Second Vatican Council, and his writings had a formative influence on those who would later become bishops of the council. While some aspects of his teaching are very much from their own time and could be rethought, one also finds in his writings a wisdom that is expansive, confident and of permanent value, deeply relevant to us today. As we approach the centenary of his death in 1923 this seems an especially apt time to revisit this spiritual legacy and reap further benefits.

The life of Blessed Columba Marmion

Family and education

Joseph Marmion was born in 1858 in Queen Street, Dublin. He grew up in a devoutly religious family and was educated by the Jesuits at Belvedere College, where he ranked among the best pupils.

Joseph's parents encouraged him from an early age in the direction of the priesthood, and at the age of seventeen he began his seminary training at Holy Cross College, Clonliffe. Joseph did well in his seminary studies; he was a lively, popular student who managed to combine a deep reverence for God with an infectious sense of humour.

A call to the priesthood

In 1897 Dr William Walsh, Archbishop of Dublin, sent Joseph to complete his theological studies in Rome, where he again excelled. The attraction of diocesan priesthood gave expression to his desire to bring the Gospel into the lives of others, an instinct which remained with him for his whole life. On the other hand a desire to live the monastic life was awoken within him when he made a visit to the Abbey of Montecassino, founded by St Benedict. Later, on a journey back to Ireland, he stopped at the recently built Benedictine Abbey of Maredsous in Belgium, where the monastic life struck a deep chord within him. The impression this place made on him never left him, and was to result in a major change of direction further down the road.

Joseph decided, together with his archbishop, that he should continue for the moment on the path towards diocesan priesthood. He was ordained to the priesthood on 16 June 1881. He was appointed curate in the parish of Dundrum. A change of appointment then brought him back to Clonliffe College, where he taught philosophy, acting also as chaplain to the Redemptoristine sisters in Drumcondra, and the women prisoners in Mountjoy prison.

Monastic life

The call to monastic life remained very much alive and finally, at the age of twenty-eight, he became a novice at Maredsous in November 1886. He was given the name Columba, a name that linked him over the centuries to another Irishman who had left his homeland to live the monastic life elsewhere: St Columba of Iona.

The personal change required to adapt to a very different life and a very different culture made deep, painful demands on the young novice, but he persevered and made his Solemn Profession.

From early in his monastic life, Fr Columba showed a gift for communication. There was a growing demand for talks and retreats from this new Irish monk. In 1890, although he was only four years in the monastery, Fr Columba was made prior of a newly founded dependent monastery at Louvain, where he also taught theology and gave spiritual direction. During those years he gave spiritual talks each week to the monks in his care. The content of these talks were later put together to form three books which were to become spiritual classics for a whole generation: *Christ, the Life of the Soul*; *Christ In His Mysteries* and *Christ, the Ideal of the Monk*.

Abbot Columba

In 1909 the position of abbot of Maredsous became vacant, and the monks of the monastery elected Fr Columba to replace him. Within a few years a major upheaval was, of course, set off by the outbreak of the First World War, which called for extraordinary measures on the part of the new abbot. At one point he left Belgium, disguised as a labourer, in search of a place of refuge for his junior monks, eventually finding a haven for them at Edermine, near Enniscorthy, Co. Wexford. From this time onwards, Abbot Columba's health began a slow decline. By January 1923 it had deteriorated to the extent that he received the last sacraments, and on Tuesday 30 January he breathed his last. Abbot Columba had dreamed of bringing Benedictine life back to Ireland by founding a monastery in his native land. Although he never did this in his lifetime, the Abbey of Maredsous did send a small group of Belgian monks to Ireland four years after his death. They set up their monastery in the recently vacated nineteenth-century castle formerly owned by the Barrington family in Murroe, County Limerick. That community remains today as Glenstal Abbey, whose patrons are Saints Joseph and Columba.

Beatified

The cause of Dom Columba towards beatification, and possible canonisation, was begun in Maredsous in 1955. In 1966 Mrs Patricia Bitzan, of St Cloud, Minnesota, was suffering with breast cancer which then spread to her lungs. After praying at Columba's tomb she was cured. In the 1990s, after a thorough investigation of the medical records and the circumstances surround the cure, officials in the Vatican concluded that this was indeed a miraculous healing, ascribing it to the intercession of Dom Columba. On 3 September 2000 he was beatified by Pope John Paul II.

The impact of Columba's teaching

Columba's writings were immensely popular: the first edition of *Christ, the Life of the Soul*, 2,500 copies, sold out in four weeks; by 1953, 200,000 copies had been sold in French and 40,000 in Italian; it was translated into nine languages altogether; the first editions of all three books were also published in braille. Columba clearly had a message that was joyfully taken up across the globe.

This book

This book will follow in outline the content of talks given by Columba to the monks at Louvain when he was Prior there. These were written up by his hearers and published under the title *Christ, the Life of the Soul*. Some readers with acute theological sensitivity may wonder about the order of the chapters. For example, why does the chapter on the Holy Spirit come after chapters on the sacraments and the Church? The chapters as they stand simply follow Columba's own order, probably influenced by theological emphases of his own time.

Some of the theological language and terminology used by Columba may sound quite foreign, even incomprehensible, to readers today. Even if his message is important, his books are, at times, a heavy read. So this book will be an effort to 'translate' his teaching into an idiom that is more accessible today and to summarise its main ideas in a shorter format.

It is also important to remember that while some of Columba's teaching is found in the documents of Vatican II, the council also developed new ways of expressing traditional ideas, with important consequences for theology and spirituality. I believe it would be a disservice simply to pass on Marmion's teaching without pointing out that, in line with mainstream Catholic theology of today, some of his teaching is open to improvement, especially in the light of Vatican II. While his teaching was good, it wasn't perfect. He was open to the currents of his day, and also very much a man of the Church; he would like us, I think, to be open to theological currents of our own time and to take on board more recent Church teaching. So this book will also point out some issues that could be rethought, or more recent teaching that might be considered by way of supplement, drawing especially on the documents of Vatican II and the *Catechism of the Catholic Church* as authoritative statements of Church teaching.

CHAPTER ONE

Christ our Holiness

It is extremely important … to know as perfectly as possible the Divine idea of holiness; to examine with the greatest care, so as to adapt ourselves to it, the plan traced out by God Himself, whereby we may attain to Him: it is only at this price that our salvation and sanctification can be realised.[1]

Blessed Columba Marmion didn't found a new religious order like St Francis of Assisi, or give a new devotion to the Church like St Faustina, nor was he martyred. Aside from some very courageous moments during the First World War, his life was not so dramatic. But he was beatified by Pope Saint John Paul II in the year 2000. So what was so holy about him? What is holiness? Before he became a Benedictine monk he ministered for a while as chaplain to a mental hospital for the criminally insane in Dundrum, Co. Dublin and remarked in one of his letters that among the residents were people of great holiness. What did he *mean* by holiness? This question, fundamental to Columba's thinking, prompted him to begin his foundational book *Christ, the Life of the Soul* by outlining the plan of our holiness and explaining how it comes about.

The big picture: God's plan for our holiness

For Columba, a first step in understanding what we mean by holiness is to realise that the more we adhere to God with firmness and stability, and the more detached we are from all that is not God, the more holy we will be. This reminds me of the words of Jesus himself: 'Whoever loves father or mother more than me is not worthy of me; and whoever loves son or daughter more than me is not worthy of me' (Mt 10:37). I might add that such holiness, paradoxically, makes us *more* loving of other people, and more appreciative of the good things of creation, not less. Adhering to God, who is love, makes us more loving, and opens our eyes to the beauty of God's work in the world and in others.

Our model of holiness: the Holy Trinity

But Christian holiness goes much further. Very early in his discussion of holiness, Columba plunged straight into Trinitarian theology. Some people see such talk only as the 'honour's course' for 'intellectuals', but it is absolutely central to an understanding of Christian holiness, and is deeply embedded in the New Testament itself.

By way of introduction to Columba's doctrine of the Trinity, we might take, as a helpful analogy, the notion of 'self-image', which is widespread nowadays in popular psychology: a person can have a 'poor self-image' or a 'positive self-image'. Our self-image can be way off-mark, thinking far too highly of ourselves, or putting ourselves down unnecessarily. We are all, to some extent, wide of the mark in our self-knowledge. Similarly, none of us is capable of perfect self-expression. What I think, feel, say and do never quite captures who I really am, but with God it is different: God's self-image is perfect.

Columba's teaching on the Holy Trinity began with God as Father, who begets the Son.[2] The Son is the self-knowledge and self-expression of the Father and, being infinitely perfect, in fact shares fully the nature of the Father in all that he is. The Son is the perfect image of the Father. The whole reality of the Father is given to the Son, except for Fatherhood. The Son receives all that he is from the Father. To quote the Nicene Creed, he is 'God from God, light from light, true God from true God'. The mutual self-giving and receiving in love between Father and Son in love is the person of the Holy Spirit. The Holy Spirit is divine love in person. God is one, and all three divine persons are God, equal in divinity.

Holiness in God can be seen as the unity in love and self-donation that exists between the three persons of the Holy Trinity. The infinite perfection of each person of the Trinity draws forth, one might say, an infinite love of the other. The genius of Columba's treatment of holiness is to say, further, that holiness for human beings is not simply to adhere to God as our creator, but to do so *as God does in the inner life of the Trinity*, to know and love God as Father, Son and Spirit know one another, to the extent that God gives us a share in divine life. We are called to share in the mutual delight and love of Father, Son and Holy Spirit insofar as we are made able for this.

For Columba, holiness was about sharing in some way the life and relational love of the persons of the Holy Trinity. He explained that this extraordinary gift is given to us in the incarnation of the Son of God.

God's plan for our holiness is realised in the incarnation

In the incarnation, the created humanity of Christ is united to his divinity so closely that there is but one person, with two natures, divine and human. He is one with God in his divinity and one with us in our humanity. Columba was fond of quoting the *Gloria* of the Mass, where it says of Christ, 'You alone are the Holy One'. It means that our holiness is a sharing in the holiness of Christ. Although we play our own part, holiness doesn't come from us but from Christ 'who became for us wisdom from God, and righteousness and sanctification and redemption' (1 Cor 1:30). This quotation from Saint Paul is central to Columba's teaching on holiness. Growth in holiness is increased participation in the divine life that is in Christ.

Our divine adoption

The core of Columba's spiritual teaching, for which he is most remembered, is that our holiness in Christ comes about through the gift of adoption. It's not a new idea – it's in the New Testament, after all – but he gave it special emphasis. Although we are not of course members of the Holy Trinity we were created to share in the life of the Holy Trinity, just as in ordinary life a person can be adopted into a family, sharing in all that belongs to the family and its relationships. This idea goes even further than the analogy of human adoption: it's not just a legal reassignment of family identity, on paper as it were, allotting a new status to us; it is something that really happens to us in who we are. Columba's writings outline how we grow into this identity in practice.

    Such is then in its majestic range and merciful simplicity, God's plan for us. *God wills our holiness,* He wills it because He loves us infinitely, and we ought to will it with him. He wills to make us saints *in making us participate in His very life,* and for that end, He *adopts us as His children,* and the heirs of His infinite glory and beatitude. But God only gives us this adoption *through His Son, Jesus Christ.* It is in Him, and by Him, that God wills to unite Himself to us, and that we should be united to Him.[3]

    Our holiness is to consist in *adhering to God, known and loved,* not only as the Author of creation, *but as He knows and loves himself* in the bliss of His Trinity; this is to be united to God to the point of sharing His intimate life.[4]

    As this love is divine, the gift of it makes us so likewise. God loves divinely; He gives Himself. We are called to receive this Divine communication in an ineffable measure. God intends to give Himself to us, not only as supreme beauty, to be the object of our contemplation, but to unite Himself to us so as to make Himself, as far as possible, one with us.[5]

ജ

NOTES

1   CLS, p. 36.

2   For more recent teaching on the meaning of the word 'Father' as applied to God, see CCC, 239–40.

3   CLS, p. 49.

4   CLS, p. 42.

5   CLS, p. 43.

CHAPTER TWO

Christ our Model of Holiness

🙞 It is this which properly constitutes the Christian: first of all to share *by sanctifying grace*, in the Divine filiation of Christ: that is the imitation of Jesus in His *state* of Son of God; and next to reproduce *by our virtues* the characteristics of this unique archetype of perfection: that is the imitation of Jesus *in his works*. St Paul points out this when he tells us we must form Christ in us [Gal 4:9], put on Christ [Rom 13:14], and bear in us the image of Christ [1 Cor 15:49].[1]

Writing to a young woman who was struggling to discover her vocation, Blessed Columba said that God didn't want us to love him like angels, 'without heart, sentiments or affections', but to love him humanly. 'We are neither spirits nor ghosts, but human beings, and we cannot go higher than perfect humanity elevated by grace. Now Jesus is perfect humanity, perfect Deity.'[2] This chapter explores Columba's teaching on Jesus as our model. We are human beings called to share the divine life of Christ, who is both human and divine. Our sharing in divine life is God's gift and we are simply asked to cooperate. Columba is at pains to point out that God's plan for us is simple and magnificent, and if we follow it, instead of finding our lives cramped and stilted, we will discover our hearts expanding with love. God's plan for us is simpler and more effective than anything we could come up with.

Jesus reveals God to us

But how can I get to know God? The first step for Columba is to realise that Jesus himself is the revelation of God. This is expressed forcefully in the Gospel according to John (Jn 14:9). Jesus says, 'If you know me, you will know my Father also. From now on you do know him and have seen him.' A little later he says, 'Whoever has seen me has seen the Father.' Columba would have us repeat these words to ourselves as we consider the various moments in the life of Jesus from the very beginning: the child in the manger, the teacher of the crowds, the one who heals, the one who reaches out to sinners, the one who hungers and thirsts, who is betrayed, humiliated and put to death while he forgives his executioners, who rises from the dead and shares with us his Holy Spirit. 'Whoever sees me sees the Father!' If we want to know what God is like, all we have to do is look at Jesus.

Jesus is our model

Jesus is perfect God and the perfect human being. He taught with unheard-of authority, even above the Jewish law, and divine power in him healed the sick; he forgave sins, which only God was supposed to do; he asked for extraordinary personal loyalty; after he was crucified he was seen by his disciples, and they were filled with the power of the Holy Spirit. It dawned on the disciples that this man was divine, and this is fundamental to Christian faith.

The disciples' intuitions about the divinity of Jesus were not arrived at simply by logical deduction, assembling the facts and arriving at a conclusion. According to Columba, intuitions of this kind are a gift from God. When Peter began to discover who Jesus really was, Jesus said, 'Flesh and blood has not revealed this to you, but my Father in heaven' (Mt 16:17). Later intuitions are shown to be a gift of the Holy Spirit: 'I still have many things to say to you, but you cannot bear them now. When the Spirit of truth comes, he will guide you into all the truth … he will take what is mine and declare it to you' (Jn 16:12-14).

Columba pointed out that, as a real human being, Jesus experienced a wide range of human experiences: friendship, grief, frustration, hunger, thirst, fatigue, compassion, joy and, above all, love. He was for most of his life so like other ordinary people that, when he preached with power in his own hometown, the locals were scandalised that this carpenter, whose family was well known to them, should speak in such a manner (Mk 6:1-3; Lk 4:22). The humanity of Jesus is, however, the gateway to our knowledge of his divinity.

Jesus is our model in who he is

When we look to Jesus as our model our first instinct may be to examine ways in which we can behave like him, as recounted in the gospels. But Columba first takes the discussion to a much deeper level: Jesus is our model not just in what he does but, firstly *in who he is*. Columba began with the divinity of Jesus. This may come as something of a surprise. Whatever about being human, divinity seems a step too far. Columba said, 'Christ is the Son of God by nature and by right, in virtue of the union of the Eternal Word with human nature; we are so by adoption and grace, but we are so really and truly.'[3] This is God's gift to us, and the word most commonly used to describe the gratuity of God's largesse towards us is 'grace'. Speaking of sanctifying grace he says 'it is the same grace that both fills the created soul of Jesus and deifies us'.[4] Jesus is fully human and divine, such that in union with him our humanity comes to its fulfilment, with a sharing in God's own life.

Jesus is our model in how he lives and acts

The next step for Columba is to examine how we live and act, again taking Christ as our model. Perhaps the best approach to modelling our lives on Christ, and one advocated by Columba, would be to take time each day to open the pages of the Gospels, where we will see all we need. In addition, we can consider certain aspects of Christ's life which he singled out as particularly important.

Above all, there is the love of Jesus for the Father. His whole life is oriented towards the Father, visible to a surprising degree already at the age of twelve when found in the temple by his parents: 'Why were you searching for me? Did you not know that I must be in my Father's house?' (Lk 2:49).[5] He seeks only what is pleasing to the Father (Jn 8:9) and his food is to do the will of the Father (Jn 4:34).

Humility

Columba also recalls the words of Jesus in St Matthew's Gospel: 'Learn from me; for I am gentle and humble in heart' (Mt 11:29). Jesus could have invited us to imitate his healing ministry, his eloquent teaching, his simple lifestyle or his courage in the face of opposition. These other aspects of his life are replicated in the lives of Christians, but more fundamental is his humility, and closely allied is his patience. Columba required both virtues when he made the move towards monastic life. From being a brilliant academic in Rome and a seminary professor in Dublin, he had to become a beginner all over again as a novice in Maredsous, with a new way of life to be learnt, a new language and a new culture. Having successfully completed his noviciate, he was asked by the novice master what was the most difficult part of the experience. His answer was, 'You, father!'

By way of conclusion, we can consider for a moment the titles of three books in which Columba's talks to his monks were put together for a wider audience: *Christ, the Life of the Soul; Christ In His Mysteries* and *Christ, the Ideal of the Monk.* The second of these goes through the liturgical year, showing how the events of Christ's life, death and resurrection are the model for our lives. But the other two titles hint that this modelling is not just an external imitation of what Jesus did and said. The deeper reality is the life of Christ himself actually at work in us. He shared our humanity that we might share his divinity.

৪১ God takes our nature so as to unite it to Himself in a personal union. What is God going to give us in return? … He could not take upon Himself our nature without a motive worthy of Him. What the Word Incarnate gives in return to humanity is an incomprehensible gift; it is a participation, real and intimate, in His Divine nature: *He hath made us partakers of His divinity.* In exchange for the humanity which He takes, the Incarnate Word gives us a share in His Divinity; He makes us partakers of His Divine Nature. And thus is accomplished the most wonderful exchange which could be made.[6]

৪১ Never let us forget that all Christian life, all holiness, is being by grace what Jesus is by nature: the Son of God. It is this that makes the sublimity of our religion. The source of all the greatness of Jesus, the source of all the value of His states, of the fruitfulness of all His mysteries, is His Divine generation and His quality of Son of God. In the same way the saint who is the highest in heaven is the one who here below was most perfectly a child of God, who has made the grace of supernatural adoption in Jesus Christ fructify the most.[7]

৪১

NOTES
1   CLS, p. 65.
2   SW, p. 1078.
3   CLS, p. 59.
4   CLS, p. 49. A fuller expression of this teaching is found in the Catechism (CCC, 1996–9).
5   An alternative version is, 'be about my Father's interest'.
6   *Christ in His Mysteries*, SW, p. 396.
7   *Christ in His Mysteries*, SW, p. 353.

CHAPTER THREE

Christ our Atonement

When St Paul exposes the Divine Plan, he says it is in Christ that 'we have redemption through His Blood, the remission of sins, according to the riches of His grace, which superabounded in us'. We have at our disposal all the riches acquired by Jesus; through Baptism they have become ours.[1]

In the final year of his life, Blessed Columba confided to his sister about his own sense of weakness and unworthiness before God adding that, 'I keep looking all the time, not at my misery so much as at his infinite Mercy. Just like a little girl who having fallen into a pool of dirty mud, runs to her mother showing her pinafore and crying until it is cleaned.'[2] Having first outlined God's plan for our divine adoption in Jesus, Columba continues by demonstrating the triumph of Christ's infinite mercy over sin in our lives.

Christ frees us from the contagion of sin
Even if God's plan is to draw us into the divine life of the Holy Trinity, there is one major problem: so often we refuse the gifts of God, we refuse God himself, and even seem incapable of getting out

of this negative pattern. The word for this is sin. It has been there since humans first walked the earth, and it seems to be contagious. Not only do we sin personally but it seems that, from the beginning, we have been born into a humanity that has gotten caught in the trap. We are far more connected with one another than we realise, in a way that has been usefully compared to the internet. With the first human 'no' to God, it was as if someone hit the download button and didn't merely install sin in himself but in all humanity, and sin spread through the entire network.[3] We are born into a broken network, and we add our own fractures to the situation. The idea of a 'broken network' or a 'fractured humanity' is a contemporary way of describing what is traditionally called 'Original Sin'. Columba, following the biblical narrative of Adam and Eve more literally, sees original sin as a loss, for Adam and all his descendants, of all right to the divine life and inheritance.

The wonderful news, and the core of the Gospel, is that, in Christ, we are given freedom from sin, and we are reconciled with God. How does Columba describe it?

St Anselm's teaching on atonement

Columba adopts the teaching of St Anselm (d. 1109), a Benedictine monk, later Archbishop of Canterbury, who sought to explain why it was necessary for God to become human.[4] A condensed version of this is that sin placed humanity over our heads in debt to God. The degree of an offence is related not only to what has been done, but also to the one whose justice has been violated. By way of contemporary analogy we could compare two forms of vandalism: if you were to go out onto a street and burn the photograph of a neighbour, it would be quite an insult, but in some countries, to burn instead the national flag would be a much bigger offence that could land you in jail, because the insult is to the whole nation. Since God is infinite, the debt against justice incurred by sin is also infinite, according to Anselm. Furthermore, since we already owe all that we have and are to God, we have absolutely nothing in addition to offer by way of just recompense, even were the debt only finite. The payment of our debt is clearly beyond us, and the solution is for God to become a human being. The obedience, unto death, of Christ has infinite value because he is God and, rendered to God, pays our debt because he is also human. Christ merits our justification before God. The idea of 'merit' here refers to something to which a person has a right. According to the approach of Anselm, and later St Thomas Aquinas, whose theology was being promoted with renewed energy when Columba was a student, we have no right to life with God because of sin; we have forfeited it. But the value before God of what Jesus has done is infinite, and he shares it with us; he shares with us his rights before the Father, his merits. Thus Columba can say of Jesus, 'Being God, His merit will have infinite value, the satisfaction will be adequate, the reparation complete.'[5] The word 'satisfaction' in this context means that the demands of justice have been satisfied. But it's not just about justice; it's also mercy, because God is the one who provides the solution as a gift to us, becoming one of us and dying our death. This approach is compatible with some of the language which the New Testament uses when it speaks of the mystery of our being saved by Christ. But this is not the only possible approach, and indeed it may not even be the best. Maybe we can consider moving beyond what Columba is saying.

A broader approach than that of St Anselm

There are dangers in the idea of saying that the death of Jesus was required to satisfy our infinite debt before God. One can easily slip into thinking that God demanded the death of his Son as a kind of blood-price, or that Jesus had to do something drastic to change God's mind about us. It also focusses almost exclusively on his death, as if it were the only thing that mattered.

The Catechism on the other hand speaks of the 'Paschal mystery of Christ's death and resurrection' (CCC, 571) thus linking his death and resurrection together as a single mystery of God's love. The Catechism also shows the necessity of understanding his death in the context of his life (CCC, 573 ff.), taking a full twenty-two articles to explore this. His death is, in fact, inseparable from his resurrection, and from his whole earthly life.[6] Our being reconciled with God is woven into the whole life-death-and-resurrection of Christ as a single mystery of God's love. Thus St Maximus of Constantinople, writing approximately three hundred years before St Anselm, can say, even of the birth of Jesus: 'Now that the divine power dwells in human nature, it will heal it and restore it to its pristine state.'[7] And even Columba agrees that *every* act of Jesus has infinite value, not just his death.

We have to be very careful about the idea that God might have deliberately wanted Jesus to suffer as much as possible (and St Anselm's treatise speaks along these lines). Let's look closely at the preaching of St Peter, as given in the Acts of the Apostles: 'This man, handed over to you according to the definite plan and foreknowledge of God, you crucified and killed' (Acts 2:23). A careful examination of the text distinguishes God's and our roles. God gave Jesus to us; but we crucified him. God willed that Jesus would bring divine love into the world in the flesh, responding to sin and evil with love, forgiveness and humility at every step, because this is God's way. Love, forgiveness and humility led to his death, as explained by the Catechism, and continued through his death into resurrection. God's plan was to give Jesus entirely and humbly to us, handed over to us, so to speak, but it was human beings who responded by having him crucified.

Jesus went through this terrible journey with the same love, forgiveness and humility that marked his whole life, right up to the end. Thus his death completed the giving of a life, totally and divinely. Columba, who retraced the final steps of this journey every day of his adult life by doing the Stations of the Cross, said something similar: 'Christ's sacrifice, begun at the moment of the Incarnation, is now achieved.'[8] It is a gift offered to us and to the Father. It reveals the horror of sin and the love made visible in God the Son. The cross stands at a pivotal moment in the mystery of Christ, revealing dramatically a forgiving love that was there all along. The blood of Christ is the culminating expression of God's mercy in the earthly life of Jesus. This is not, however, the same as saying that God required a debt to be paid.

Images other than paying a debt

It might be useful to know that when St Anselm developed his treatment of this topic, he was trying to provide an argument that Christians could use to convince non-Christians, and for this reason he deliberately chose not to base it on ideas from the New Testament. A weakness here is that, instead of being grounded in the word of God, his theory is based instead on the notions of justice and honour prevalent in his own time and culture. But when we look to the New Testament we find a wealth of wonderful language to describe our salvation. It uses many images and metaphors to describe the mystery of our freedom from sin in Christ. He is like a strong man who has burgled the devil's house; he is the shepherd who carries home the lost sheep; he is the doctor who heals the sick; he is like the sacrifices offered in the temple for sin; he is like the Passover lamb whose blood was a sign of God's protection on life's journey; entering heaven itself, he is like the Jewish High Priest who entered the Holy of Holies to intercede for the people and proclaim their forgiveness; just as Moses used a blood ceremony to symbolise the life-bond between God and his people, so the blood of Christ is a new and everlasting covenant; he is the new Adam, a new beginning for the human family; he is like the blood-relative who rescues you, vindicates your rights, even buys you out of slavery. This last image is the image of 'redemption' – being bought out of slavery, but dominant in this biblical metaphor is the idea of God buying us for himself. In the New Testament, 'there is never [any] question of a person who demands or receives payment of a price'.[9] While Columba draws on many of these biblical texts, he links them all back to the idea of paying a debt, but it doesn't have to work that way. They can stand on their own as alternative expressions of our salvation in Christ, a mystery that is no doubt beyond any single explanation.

Atonement

Atonement means that in Christ we are made one with God (at-one-ment). Like branches on the vine, we can be united to Christ, who is without sin and whose life is stronger than death, so that his life is ours. Whenever we may feel in debt to God because of sin, Columba's fundamental message is that in God's eyes there is no debt, aside from the joyful debt of gratitude for the generosity of his forgiveness brought to us in Christ, which is always available – we can believe this whether or not we buy into the logic of St Anselm espoused by Columba. A favourite image of Columba's is that of our leaning on Christ, since our being at rights with God comes from him. He makes us holy.

 ₞ All the actions accomplished by the humanity of Christ, however small, simple or limited they may be in their physical reality and earthly duration, are attributed to the Divine Person to whom this humanity is joined; they are the actions of a God ... they acquire ... an inestimable price, infinite value and inexhaustible efficacy.[10]

 ₞ God's plan for the redemption and Sanctification of the world is just the opposite of what we would have thought. We should have expected that God would have come into this world in great power and majesty, and, surrounded by a group of learned men, convert the world. But no. He came as a *poor, weak* little infant; He lives in obscurity and labours for years; then then is murdered by men who seem to have conquered Him, and defy Him to come down from the Cross. His whole work is ruined; and His reputation blasted. And it is then that He conquers! It is the triumph of weakness for 'what is weak in God is stronger than all men's strength; what is folly in God is greater than all men's wisdom, in order that now flesh may take glory to itself' [2 Cor 1:27-9]. This is God's way. And on Easter Sunday I *saw* that it was the divine triumph of God's weakness.[11]

ঞ

NOTES

1   CLS, p. 77.

2   Letter to his sister Rosie, SW, p. 990.

3   Shayne Looper, 'It's Not the Way It's Supposed to Be', *The Coldwater Daily Reporter*, 9 September 2017, archived at https://shaynelooper.com/2017/09/09/its-not-the-way-its-supposed-to-be/, accessed 22 September 2022.

4   This teaching on atonement was passed on by Thomas Aquinas, to whom Columba referred directly in his writing.

5   CLS, p. 68.

6   The Catechism does however have different strands of theology at work and, in another context, does speak of Christ's meriting our justification through his passion and death (CCC, 1992), which is compatible with St Anselm's theory. The book wasn't written all by one person and has a number of different theologies at work in different sections.

7   From the Fifty Centuries of St Maximus, 1, 8–13, quoted in Maxwell E. Johnson (ed.), *Benedictine Daily Prayer: A Short Breviary* (Dublin: Columba Press, 2005), p. 82.

8   CIHM, p. 489.

9   Stanislas Lyonnet, 'Redemption' in Xavier Leon-Dufour (ed.), *Dictionary of Biblical Theology* (1962). Revised edition, 1968. English translation, 1973 (London: Geoffrey Chapman Publishers), p. 482.

10   CLS, p. 69.

11   Letter to the Poor Clare Colettines of Cork, SW, p. 1102.

Christ and his Sacraments

  They are, indeed, true and pure sources as well as inexhaustible ones where we shall infallibly find the Divine life with which Christ Jesus is filled and of which He wills to make us partakers. *I am come that they may have life.*[1]

Always important in Catholic life and tradition, the sacraments featured prominently in Columba's own life. Born on Holy Thursday, 1 April 1858, he was baptised five days later on Dublin's Arran Quay, in the church of St Paul, whose message would form such an important part of his teaching. After making his first Holy Communion, he went to Mass daily, and during holiday time he never passed a church without going in to pray before the Blessed Sacrament. In the sacraments he also served others as a priest, ordained on the feast of Corpus Christi. He received the Eucharist on the very last day of his life. His life was encompassed by the sacraments.

In Chapter Four of *Christ, the Life of the Soul*, Columba described the human encounter with divine life: in the earthly life of Jesus, in the sacraments, and in the faith that enables us to meet Christ anywhere and everywhere.

Through the humanity of Jesus to his divinity

When people met Jesus in his earthly life, they did not just meet a great teacher, a person of immense compassion, a healer and a fine human being; they encountered God in and through the humanity of Jesus. People kept trying to touch Jesus because 'power came out from him and healed them all' (Lk 6:19). His divinity was present to people in and through his humanity.

Columba also pointed out that Jesus' divine power healed not only on a physical level but also – more importantly – on a spiritual level. When he healed a paralysed man, Jesus did so in order to convince onlookers of the truth of the spiritual healing which had come from his words, 'Take heart, son, your sins are forgiven' (Mt 9:2). The question then arises as to how it might be for us today: is there a way of meeting the divinity of Christ that is equally well adapted to our humanity in our own time? Columba pointed to the sacraments as an all-important place of divine-human encounter, encouraging his readers vigorously to participate in them.

Meeting Christ in the sacraments

Christ can act in our lives in a variety of ways, but as Columba pointed out, the sacraments are particularly important points of contact with him. The *Catechism of the Catholic Church* develops and reinforces this idea:

> Sacraments are 'powers that come forth' from the Body of Christ,[2] which is ever-living and life-giving. They are actions of the Holy Spirit at work in his Body, the Church. They are 'the masterworks of God' in the new and everlasting covenant. (CCC, 1116)

The power of the sacrament then does not come from the celebrant or the recipient of the sacrament, but from Christ himself. This is important to remember, especially in moments where all is less than ideal in a particular celebration, be it the attitude of the priest or of others present, and all the more so if people's lives contradict what they say and do in the sacraments. The power of Christ is bigger than all of this, and he still acts, even through unworthy ministers. Columba repeated words from St Augustine, who – as a great orator – put it rather dramatically: 'It is Christ who baptises; Judas baptises, it is Christ Who does so.'[3]

The importance of our own response to Christ in the sacraments

Christ is always active in the sacraments, regardless of the worthiness or otherwise of those who minister. But the sacraments, like any moment of encounter, are a two-way process. It is not enough for Christ to offer us his love; we must also be willing to receive it. It is in fact possible for us to close the door in the face of what is on offer. It is not enough for a gift to be given; it must also be received. For example: attendance at Mass simply as an act of social conformity, without any real openness to the reality of what is unfolding in the liturgy, falls short of a willingness to receive the particular gift of love that is celebrated.

Columba regretted that too many people participate in the sacraments half-heartedly, not realising their greatness. Today we could further develop his thought by drawing on the teaching of the Second Vatican Council and say: notice that Christ is present in the congregation when you gather and pray together; notice that Christ works through the priest, for all his limitations; notice that Christ calls to your heart through the readings; notice that Christ is present in the sacramental rite itself, especially the Holy Eucharist.[4] Columba was vividly aware of these aspects of the sacraments in his own life.

He also pointed to the need to remove anything in our lives that might be at odds with God's action in the sacraments (we can think of our own examples: dishonesty, gossip, greed, etc.):

> Dam up a river, the water cannot pass; raise the floodgate, the water will rush forth. So it is with the grace of the sacraments; there is in them all that is necessary for their action; yet it is also necessary that grace should not meet with any obstacle in us.[5]

Columba insisted on the importance of the sacraments. It is true that God is absolutely free, and is not bound to the sacraments as the only way of helping us. The most ordinary events can be moments of illumination and inspiration. On the other hand, as he pointed out, people have been known to be profoundly mistaken about states of intense feeling or altered perception, thinking that these point to divine intervention. The sacraments are normally less dramatic, humbly adapted to our personal and social nature and deep, authentic sources of spiritual life. Columba assures us that in the sacraments we are on secure ground.

From the sacraments to Christian living

As regards the continued contact between Christ and us in the *living out* of the sacraments, Columba highlighted the importance of faith, referring to the healing of the woman who had a flow of blood for twelve years.[6] She believed that even to touch Jesus' clothes would be enough to bring her healing. She touched his garment and Jesus became aware of healing power that had gone out of him. Jesus was in the middle of a crowd that was pressing in on him from all sides, so physical touch was not really the issue. Jesus knew that it was not just the touch, but the woman's faith that healed her: 'Daughter, your faith has made you well.' Columba's choice of this event as an encouragement for our own faith is particularly apt: the fact that we cannot perceive Jesus physically in the way his contemporaries in Palestine did is no hindrance to our real contact with him. Our faith in Jesus is what connects us to him and to his saving power. Columba would have us realise this can happen at any moment, but especially in the sacraments.

୨ଠ When, then, in reading the Gospel, we ponder in our minds the words and actions of Our Lord; when in prayer, or in meditation, we contemplate His virtues; above all, when we associate with the Church in the celebration of His mysteries (as I shall show later); when we unite ourselves to Him in each of our actions, whether we eat or work, or do any action indifferent in itself in union with the like actions that He himself accomplished when He lived here below, when we do this with faith and love, with humility and confidence, there is then a strength, a power, a Divine virtue, which goes out from Christ to enlighten us, to help us remove obstacles to His Divine operations in us, so as to produce grace in our souls.[7]

℘ We see in the Saints marvels of Divine generosity, from the *charisma* which illustrate the times of the early Christians to the wonderful favours which, even in our days, abound in so many souls: *God is wonderful in his saints.* But in this matter Christ has made no promise to anyone; He has not indicated these means as the regular way, either of salvation, or even of holiness, whilst He has instituted the sacraments, with their particular energies and efficacious virtues; hence they constitute, in their harmonious variety, the whole means of sure salvation. Here there is no illusion possible, and we know how dangerous are illusions created by the devil in matters of piety and sanctity![8]

℘

NOTES

1   CLS, p. 82.

2   Cf. Lk 5:17; 6:19; 8:46.

3   St Augustine, *Tract. In Johann.*, VI, quoted by Blessed Columba in CLS, p. 84.

4   See the Constitution on the Sacred Liturgy, *Sacrosanctum concilium*, 7.

5   CLS, p. 83.

6   A footnote in Columba's text refers to Lk 8:43-8. The importance of faith is even clearer in the account in the Gospel according to Mark (5:21-43).

7   CLS, p. 89.

8   CLS, p. 86. The idea of the 'institution of the sacraments by Christ' did not mean for Columba that he instituted them all directly in all their details. Christ was however their author and unique source.

Christ and his Body the Church

⁊ In the silence of prayer, I see more and more clearly, and especially to-day, that the great object our Lord had in view in giving Himself to us in the Holy Eucharist was to *incorporate* us in Him as His mystical body, so that with Him and in Him, we may perfect the great work of the Father: our sanctification and the salvation of the world.[1]

Blessed Columba gave the fifth chapter of his book *Christ, the Life of the Soul* the title: 'The Church, Mystical Body of Christ'. This title implies an intimate connection between the Church and Christ, as between the body and the head, in a manner that transcends our visible, tangible world. At the same time Columba pointed to some of the very visible ways in which the Church's life and activity are manifested: in teaching, the exercise of authority, the celebration of the sacraments and other examples of the Church's worship. In examining this, it's important too to include some clarifications from Vatican II that are necessary for today's readers.

The Church as Body of Christ
To speak of the Church as the Body of Christ points to something

more profound than institutional structures. Columba said that the image of the body, drawn from St Paul, 'gives us a more profound conception of the Church in showing the intimate relations existing between her and Christ.'[2] Thus he observed that when Saul heard the voice of Christ on the road to Damascus,

> ℘ You will notice that Christ does not say: 'Why do you persecute *my disciples*?' – something He could have said with just as much truth, since He Himself had already ascended into heaven and it was only the Christians that St Paul was hunting down; but He says: 'Why do you persecute *me*?' – 'It is *I* whom you are persecuting.' Why does Christ speak in this way? Because His disciples belong to Him as His very own; because the society composed of them forms His mystical body. To persecute the souls who believe in Jesus Christ is to persecute Christ himself.[3]

Columba also quoted some striking lines from St Augustine:

> ℘ Let us congratulate ourselves, let us pour out thanksgiving: we have been made, not only Christians but Christ. Do you understand, my brethren, the grace of God towards us? Let us marvel, let us thrill with joy, we have been made Christ: he the head, we the members – the whole man, He and us … Who is the head, and who are the members? Christ and the Church.[4]

But Christ and the Church are not exactly the same. While they are spiritually one, organically related one might say, there are important distinctions. This is implicit in Columba's words, but receives little emphasis. Head and body are not quite the same thing. Other biblical images, while also expressing a close connection between Christ and the Church, make this distinction clearer: He is the shepherd and we are the flock; he is the Bridegroom and the Church is the bride.

Teaching and jurisdiction in the Church: how should it work?

Columba insisted on absolute submission to the doctrine and laws of the Church, referring to scripture passages such as 'As the Father has sent me, so I send you' (Jn 20:21) and 'Whoever who listens to you listens to me, and whoever rejects you rejects me, and whoever rejects me rejects the one who sent me' (Lk 10:16). Such absolute submission is problematic for many people today. 'Just following orders' is not enough, and conscience is highly valued. Today we are also more aware of ways in which members of the hierarchy have been deficient in their teaching and leadership, from the days of Galileo to inadequate safeguarding of children more recently.

Columba was aware of human inadequacies in the Church. Pointing to St Peter's denial of Jesus he said, 'There is a double element in the Church – a human and a Divine element. The human element is the frailty of the men who hold the power of Christ in order to direct us. Consider how weak St. Peter was!'[5]

It might be helpful to know that Columba placed particular emphasis on obedience in his own personal life. He once said, 'I became a monk in order to obey.' But Benedictine obedience is not just 'from the top down'. It is a generous two-way listening process involving abbot and community. Columba, as abbot, counselled his monks to be quite frank in this respect. A broader way of looking at hierarchy, authority and obedience is also evident in the documents of the Second Vatican Council and subsequent Church teaching.

When the overall shape of the Council document on the Church (*Lumen Gentium*) was approved, a definite decision was taken to speak firstly of the Church as a whole, the People of God, before referring to the hierarchy and their specific place and role within the Church. In article 27, bishops were exhorted to listen to those whom they serve. Later, the Catechism stressed the importance of the initiative of lay people, especially in relation to social, political and economic realities (CCC, 899). Quoting the *Code of Canon Law*, it also reiterated that lay people have a right and sometimes a duty to make their voices heard about matters which pertain to the good of the Church (CCC, 907).

In a similar vein, Pope Francis has recently initiated worldwide discussion of the synodal nature of the Church, encouraging mutual listening at all levels. Addressing a synodal gathering in Rome on this topic, he spoke about the need to hear everyone's voice in the Church:

> ∞ I want to emphasise this. This is an exercise of mutual listening, conducted at all levels of the Church and involving the entire People of God ... Listening, speaking and listening. It is not about garnering opinions, not a survey, but a matter of listening to the Holy Spirit ... The word of God journeys with us. Everyone has a part to play; no one is a mere extra. This is important: everyone has a part to play. The Pope, the Cardinal Vicar and the auxiliary bishops are not more important than the others.[6]

Salvation through the Church: what does this mean?
Columba's language in relation to salvation through the Church is strong:

> ∞ ... the absolute submission to the Church of all your being, intellect, will and energies is the only means of going to the Father.[7]

> ∞ No one goes to Christ except through the Church; we only belong to Christ if we belong in fact or in desire to the Church. It is only in the unity of the Church that we can live the life of Christ.[8]

For Catholics in Columba's time, 'Church' meant 'the Roman Catholic Church', and membership of this Church was necessary for salvation. For Columba to speak, above, about belonging to the Church in desire, and not in fact, suggests that what it means to belong to the Church is not black-and-white. In other words, some 'non-Catholics' may belong to the Church in a way that neither they nor others realise. But Columba's theology, which was very much of its time, still raises questions about the salvation of those who do not desire to be Catholics. As we look at these issues today it is very important to know that the Second Vatican Council took a much broader approach.

On the basis of what the Council said, it is possible to affirm, of other Christian denominations, 'that the Church of Christ is present and operative in the churches and ecclesial Communities not yet fully in communion with the Catholic Church, on account of the elements of sanctification and truth that are present in them'.[9]

The Council went further: it also spoke of various ways in which God provides for the salvation of many who, acting in good faith, are not in the full communion of the Church. Included among these are those preparing for baptism, Christians of other denominations, the Jewish people, Muslims, those who sincerely seek God and follow their conscience, and people with no explicit knowledge of God who strive to live a good life.[10]

Thus statements like 'there is no salvation outside the Church', need to be handled with great care. 'Re-formulated positively,' according to the Catechism, 'it means that all salvation comes from Christ the Head through the Church which is his Body' (CCC, 846). In ways known to himself, God can lead those who, through no fault of their own, are ignorant of the Gospel, to a faith that is pleasing to him.[11]

Columba would want us to believe strongly that Christ is at work in the Church, even if the process seems messy at times. Salvation comes through the Church, his body. Vatican II would have us realise that this salvation spills out across the globe to many who may seem to be going another way.

   ଚ   What we have to remember is that, here on earth, [the Church] continues the mission of Jesus by her doctrine and jurisdiction, by her Sacraments and worship.[12]

   ଚ   By her doctrine, which she guards intact and integral in a living and uninterrupted tradition; by her jurisdiction, in virtue of which she has authority to direct us in the name of Christ; by the Sacraments whereby she enables us to draw from the sources of grace which her Divine founder has created; by the worship which she herself organises so as to render all glory and honour to Jesus Christ, and to His Father.[13]

ॐ

NOTES

1 Letter of 28 October 1902, cited in Raymond Thibaut, *Abbot Columba Marmion: A Master of the Spiritual Life 1858–1923* (London and Edinburgh: Sands & Co., 1932), p. 148.

2 CLS, p. 98.

3 *Christ, the Life of the Soul*, translation by Alan Bancroft (Leominster: Gracewing Publications, 2005), p. 124. This passage is missing from the translation normally used in this book.

4 *Tract. In Johann.*, XXI, 8–9, quoted in CLS, p. 100.

5 CLS, p. 97.

6 Address to the Faithful of the Diocese of Rome, 18 September 2021, https://www.vatican.va/content/francesco/en/speeches/2021/september/documents/20210918-fedeli-diocesiroma.html, accessed 22 September 2022.

7 CLS, p. 94.

8 CLS, p. 96.

9 Congregation for the Doctrine of the Faith, 'Responses to Some Questions Regarding Certain Aspects of the Doctrine on the Church', 29 June 2007, http://www.vatican.va/roman_curia/congregations/cfaith/documents/rc_con_cfaith_doc_20070629_responsa-quaestiones_en.html, accessed 22 September 2022.

10 *Lumen Gentium*, 14–16. It is well worth looking up this text in its entirety, as it has an extraordinary breadth of vision.

11 Cf. *Ad Gentes*, 7.

12 CLS, p. 94.

13 CLS, p. 94.

CHAPTER SIX

Christ and his Spirit

§⊃ For some time I have felt more and more a special attraction towards the Holy Spirit. I have a great desire to be guided, led, moved in all things by the Spirit of Jesus. Our Lord, as Man, did nothing except under the impulsion of the Holy Spirit and under His dependence.[1]

Blessed Columba began his adult life by preparing for ordination for the diocesan priesthood, but it gradually became clear to him that his call to share the Gospel would best be lived within monastic life. This involved fresh insight and the courage to take a totally new turn in his life. It began with a visit to the monastery at Montecassino in Italy, founded by St Benedict himself. It was there he first felt that God was calling him to monastic life. A Belgian friend of his studying in Rome confided that he was considering the life of a missionary monk in Australia, and this fired Columba up with enthusiasm. Columba agreed that, on his way back to Ireland after his studies, he would meet up with this Belgian friend at the abbey of Maredsous in Belgium. The place made a huge impression on him, and the moment he crossed the threshold he had a sense that God wanted him there. Columba had, however, made a prior commitment to the Dublin diocese and further discernment with his archbishop was needed to verify this intuition and to think about the best time to make a move to Belgium. This took five years. We can say that this process was the work of the Holy Spirit in Columba's life as it unfolded. The presence and work of the Holy Spirit in each baptised person was central to Columba's own teaching in this area, and while this chapter follows the general outline of his teaching on the Holy Spirit, a broader presentation of this important topic can be found by looking at the Catechism (CCC, 683–747).

The Holy Spirit within the Trinity and in the world

Columba described the Holy Spirit as the mutual love between the Father and the Son. We might say that the Holy Spirit is 'love in person'. This love is also directed towards us. In Chapter Six of *Christ, the Life of the Soul*, before describing the work of the Holy Spirit among us, Columba made a rather technical point, but an important one nonetheless: every action done by God in the world is the work of all three persons of the Holy Trinity. He noted, however, that traditionally we often attribute such actions to just one of the divine persons. For example we might sometimes say that the Father creates, the Son redeems, the Spirit inspires, and so on. According to Columba, this is a way of honouring the distinct personhood of each divine person, but it doesn't imply that the other divine persons are any less involved in the particular action we describe. Thus we might say that the Father creates because within the Trinity the Father has the characteristic of origin, but in fact all three divine persons are involved in the work of creation. For the purposes of this chapter, when we talk about the action of the Holy Spirit in the world, this always includes the action of the Father and the Son. The Catechism says: 'The whole divine economy is the common work of the three divine persons. However, each divine person performs the common work according to his unique personal property' (CCC, 258).

The work of the Holy Spirit in the life of Jesus and in us

In the incarnation and all that flows from it, Jesus and the Holy Spirit are inseparably intertwined.

Columba taught that not only was Jesus conceived by the Holy Spirit, but since he was both human and divine, the Spirit enabled Christ's human nature to act in away befitting a divine person, producing divine fruits.

Columba spoke of the fullness of the gifts of the Spirit in Jesus, drawing upon Isaiah's messianic prophecy: 'The spirit of the Lord shall rest on him, the spirit of wisdom and understanding, the spirit of counsel and might, the spirit of knowledge and the fear of the Lord' (Is 11:2). If we look at his treatment of the Holy Spirit's gifts, this gives us a synthesis describing, in a general way, the work of the Holy Spirit both in the life of Jesus and in our lives.

Columba said, 'These marvels were operated in Christ under the inspiration of the Spirit, [and] are reproduced in us, at least in part, when we allow ourselves to be guided by this Divine Spirit. But do we possess this Spirit? Yes, without any doubt.'[2] The Holy Spirit, he said, 'loves us with an unspeakable love; He wills our sanctification; His inspirations, all proceeding from His goodness and love, have no other end than to mould us to a greater resemblance to Jesus'.[3]

The gifts of the Holy Spirit

While Columba treated each gift of the Spirit individually we should not get too worried about trying to make watertight distinctions between them. The text from Isaiah that inspired the idea of seven gifts was an attempt to describe the awaited Messiah. What is important for Christians is their cumulative effect as a description of Jesus and, by extension, of the Holy Spirit's work in us.

Sapientia is the Latin word for *wisdom*. There is a tradition going back many centuries that makes a connection with *sapor*, the Latin word for taste. 'It is,' Columba says, 'an intimate, a deep knowledge that relishes the things of God.' It gives us 'the relish for celestial and supernatural things', and is 'the response to "O taste and see that the Lord is sweet" [Ps 33:9]'.[4]

The gift of *understanding* concerns the truth of what we believe. An example given by Columba is the special insight that can come when we read scripture in a prayerful way.

Columba saw the gift of *counsel* as related primarily to how we should best act in each situation:

     ɛɔ   The soul of Jesus contemplated the Father beholding in Him the model of His works; it was the Spirit of Counsel that showed Him the desires of the Father … Sometimes, natural prudence, always limited, points out how to act in such or such a way; then, by the gift of counsel, the Holy Spirit shows higher principles of conduct which ought to direct the actions of the child of God.[5]

Knowing what is right is one thing, but having the courage and strength to act accordingly, sometimes in the face of great opposition or apparent danger, is another. The gift of *fortitude* is 'power from on high' that enables us to carry out God's will. Columba pointed to examples such as Moses standing up to Pharaoh, and the first disciples facing persecution. 'Such a one is strong with the very strength of God,' he said. 'It is this strength that makes the martyrs, and sustains the virgins. The world wonders to see them so courageous because it imagines they find their strength in themselves, while in reality they draw it from God alone.'[6]

The way each of us sees the world can be quite limited, and sometimes wide of the mark. We all have our own bias. The gift of *knowledge*, as understood by Columba, enables us to 'know the things of creation, and of ourselves, from God's point of view'. Looking at the world around us without the gift of knowledge that comes from God has been more recently compared to the way a small child sees reality when it crawls around on its hands and legs – a very limited view indeed.[7]

Columba treated the gift of *piety* and the gift of *fear* together:

     ɛɔ   This is the reverence that the Spirit places within our souls; He keeps it there but in mingling it, by the gift of piety, with that love and filial tenderness which results from our

Divine adoption and makes us cry out to God: 'Father!' This gift of piety implants in us, as in Jesus, the tendency to refer everything to our Father.[8]

As regards fear, Columba distinguished between the kind of fear a slave might have of being punished, and a 'filial fear'; the latter is a kind of reverence before the infinite perfection of God while knowing that we are, at the same time, God's beloved sons and daughters.

Our cooperation with the Holy Spirit

Columba finally encourages us to cooperate always with the Holy Spirit. We should ask for the help of the Holy Spirit, ask for a renewal of his sevenfold gift which, perhaps, may have become dormant within us. We should also thank the Holy Spirit for inspirations received.

ꙮ Souls, simple and uncultured, but upright and docile to the inspirations of the Holy Spirit, have a certitude, a comprehension of supernatural things and a penetration into them that is sometimes astonishing; they have a spiritual instinct which warns them of error and makes the hold to the revealed truth with a singular assurance protecting them from all doubts. Whence does this arrive? From study? From deep examination into the truths of their faith? No, from the Holy Spirit, the Spirit of truth who by the gift of understanding or of knowledge perfects their virtue of faith.[9]

ꙮ You read a text of Holy Scripture; you have read and re-read it many times without having been struck by it; but one day, a sudden light flashes, illuminating to its depths, so to speak, the truth set forth in this text; this truth then becomes altogether clear to you and often a principle of supernatural life and action. Is it by your reflections that you have arrived at this result? No, it is an illumination, and intuition of the Holy Spirit Who, but the gift of understanding, makes you penetrate further into the inmost and deep meaning of the revealed truths so that you may hold them the more firmly.[10]

    As I have said, the action of the Spirit in the soul is delicate because it is an action of completeness, of perfection; His touches are of infinite delicacy. We must be watchful not to oppose the workings of this Divine Spirit by our levity, our voluntary dissipation, our carelessness, or wilful deliberate resistances, by an ill-regulated attachment to our own judgement.[11]

NOTES

1   Personal notes, 3 March 1900, cited in Raymond Thibaut, *Abbot Columba Marmion: A Master of the Spiritual Life 1858–1923* (London and Edinburgh: Sands & Co., 1932), p. 398.

2   CLS, p. 110.

3   CLS, p. 115.

4   CLS, p. 115.

5   CLS, p. 116.

6   CLS, p. 117.

7   Elder Aemilianos of Simonopetra, *The Mystical Marriage: Spiritual Life according to St Maximos the Confessor*, English translation by V. Rev. Archimandrite Maximos Constas (Columbia: Newrome Press, 2018), p. 111.

8   CLS, p. 118.

9   CLS, p. 114.

10   CLS, p. 116.

11   CLS, p. 120.

CHAPTER SEVEN

Faith in Christ

On 1 February 1906 Blessed Columba wrote in his private spiritual notebook:

> ∞ 'Who is he that overcometh the world but he that believeth that Jesus is the Son of God?' The whole occupation of my life ought to be to lay down this 'ego' at the feet of Jesus and continually to see Jesus *as God, in me*, according Him with all my faculties. ... He must become the *beginning* of all my activity. ... He is wisdom, power, love; without Him, I am foolishness, weakness, selfishness: 'Without Me you can do nothing.'[1]

Here Columba was writing for himself, not for others, but what he says sums up very well the main idea of this chapter: faith in Christ. He saw it as the foundation of Christian living, and explored examples of it in scripture.

Faith: the foundation of Christian living

Having sketched out the broad dimensions of God's plan for our holiness, in the opening chapters of his book *Christ, the Life of the Soul*, Columba continued by drawing out the implications for our Christian living. The first, and foundational, element is faith. We have seen already that God's plan for us is divine adoption, whereby we share in the life of the only Son of God. Our acceptance of Christ in faith is the key to this shared life: 'To all who did accept him he gave power to become children of God, to those who believed in his name' (Jn 1:12). Columba said that our first access to God is, according to St Thomas Aquinas, through faith.

Faith: examples from scripture

In order to get a sense of what Columba meant by faith, it is helpful to look at the numerous scriptural examples to which he refers. Even better than looking at the short summaries below, one could look at the full gospel story in each case and meditate on it, discovering there a mirror of our own relationship with Christ.

Two blind men approach Jesus asking for help and he replies, 'Do you believe I can do this?' When they say, 'Lord, we do,' he touches their eyes saying, 'According to your faith, let it be done to you.' And they are healed (Mt 9:27 ff.).

A man whose son is in need of healing is challenged by Jesus: 'Everything is possible for one who has faith,' to which the man replies, 'I have faith, help my lack of faith!' Jesus heals the boy and expels an evil spirit (Mk 9:18 ff.).

A woman in search of healing pushes through a crowd in order to touch the fringe of Jesus' cloak. Jesus says to her, 'Your faith has saved you; go in peace' (Lk 7:37 ff.).

To a man who has just been told that his daughter is dead, Jesus says, 'Do not be afraid; only have faith.' Jesus goes to the man's house and raises up his daughter (Mk 5:25 ff.).

When a centurion says to Jesus, 'I am not worthy to have you under my roof; just give the word and my servant will be cured,' Jesus says to bystanders, 'In truth I tell you, in no one in Israel have I found faith as great as this' (Mt 8:5 ff.).

When a woman with a bad reputation makes a surprising display of love and appreciation to Jesus at the house of a Pharisee, Jesus says to her, 'Your faith has saved you; go in peace' (Lk 7:37 ff.).

At the end of the Gospel according to Mark, Jesus commissions his disciples to proclaim the Gospel to the whole world, saying, 'Whoever believes and is baptised will be saved' (Mk 16:16).

Having surveyed these stories in a reflective way, Columba commented: 'So then faith is the first virtue Our Lord claims from those who approach Him and it remains the same for us all.' He concludes by saying, 'Here below, God wills to be known, adored and served by faith; – and the greater, the more ardent and practical this faith is, the more we are pleasing to God.'[2]

A closer look at Christian faith

If faith is so important, what is it? Columba said that faith in another human being 'is the adhesion of our intellect to the word of another'.[3] If someone is trustworthy and reliable, we have faith in their word; we believe them and trust what they say. Faith in God 'is the adherence of our intelligence, not to the word of a man, but to the word of God. God can neither deceive nor be deceived.'[4]

Columba saw the focus of Christian faith as concentrated on one crucial aspect: the divinity of Jesus. 'One who accepts the Divinity of Christ embraces the whole revelation.'[5] For the sake of completeness one should add immediately a reference also to the humanity of Jesus, which is never in question for Columba. Since Christ is our model, a faith that recognises both his humanity and his divinity is also necessary if we are to have a balanced approach to ourselves and the living of our own lives. The divinity of Christ, in which are called to have a share, opens up the extraordinary horizon of the dignity which is ours to live. To ignore this is to close our eyes to an amazing gift from God that begins already today. To ignore his humanity on the other hand brings with it the danger of ignoring our own human limitations, which is very unwise. Columba's emphasis on the divinity of Christ is helpful but, no more than Columba, we must not lose sight of his humanity.

We can say that, because God has become human in Christ, his humanity is our path towards his divinity. Columba said, 'This little child, lying in the crib is Thy Son, I adore and give myself to Him; this Youth toiling in the workshop of Nazareth, is Thy Son, I adore Him; this Man crucified on Calvary is Thy Son, I adore Him; these fragments of bread are the appearances under which Thy Son is hidden, I there adore Him.'[6]

Relying on Christ

Columba pointed out that considerable strength and joy also come from another aspect of our faith: that we rely on Christ for our holiness. As we have already seen in Chapter Three, an awareness of the sin in our lives, of our failures and compromises, needs to be balanced with faith in Christ as the one in whom we are reconciled with God. As St Paul says, he is our wisdom, our righteousness, our holiness, our redemption (1 Cor 1:30). He makes constant intercession for us (Heb 7:25). Christ is the one who justifies us, who puts us in right relationship with God, as a free gift, not as something earned. These are central themes of Columba's teaching. Put in more personal terms, St Thérèse of Lisieux, for whom Columba had a high regard, once said that were she guilty of the worst imaginable sins, she would still have boundless confidence in God.

℘ Such is true faith, the faith that being made perfect in love, surrenders all our being, and practically enveloping all the acts, all the works of our spiritual life, constitutes the very *basis* of our supernatural edifice and of all sanctity. In order to be truly a *foundation*, it is needful that faith should sustain the works we accomplish and become the principle of all our progress in the spiritual life.[7]

℘ In the supernatural life, faith in Jesus is a power so much the more active as it is the more deeply anchored in the soul. It first embraces with fervour all the fullness of its object; and as faith refers all to Christ, it regards all things in the divine light of Christ.[8]

ဆ

NOTES

1   Private notes, 1 February 1906, cited in Raymond Thibaut, *Abbot Columba Marmion: A Master of the Spiritual Life 1858–1923* (London and Edinburgh: Sands & Co., 1932), p. 159.

2   CLS, p. 129.

3   CLS, p. 128.

4   CLS, p. 128.

5   CLS, p. 130.

6   *Christ, the Life of the Soul*, translation by Alan Bancroft (Leominster: Gracewing Publishing, 2005), p. 183.

7   CLS, p. 134.

8   CLS, p. 135.

CHAPTER EIGHT

Baptised into Christ

ᔥ   Divine life is first infused into us at Baptism. ... Baptism is the sacrament of Divine adoption and Christian initiation. At the same time we shall especially find in it, as its germ, the double aspect of 'death to sin' and 'life unto God' which ought to characterise the whole existence of a disciple of Christ.[1]

Blessed Columba's chapter on baptism has the title: 'Baptism, the Sacrament of Divine Adoption and Christian Initiation: Death and Life'. In going beyond divine adoption, he considers such topics as death to sin and life to God, rebirth, baptismal living, and questions around the necessity of baptism for salvation.

Death to sin and life to God

When water is blessed for baptism, the priest prays that 'all who have been buried in Christ by Baptism into death may rise again to life with him'. Inherent in this language is the experience of water not only as life-giving but also as destructive. Water drowns. Columba insists that there is in each one of us a way of living that must be brought to an end. Baptism drowns the sin in us. For an adult convert this experience can be more dramatic than for someone who has been baptised as an infant. For some adult converts there is a real wrench away from a former way of life, a real 'death' to undergo. But since sin creeps into all our lives, the grace of baptism needs constant renewal to put to death all that is destructive in us.

Columba evoked the baptismal rites of the early Church. These were ritual drownings that usually involved the immersion of the whole body in the baptismal pool. Candidates were stripped naked and plunged three times into the water as they professed their faith in the three persons of the Blessed Trinity, and then rose from the waters, to be clothed in white and anointed with oil. Immersion is still in fact the officially preferred form of baptism in the Church, and some modern baptisteries are being built in such a way as to make this possible again.

Drawing on St Paul, Columba pointed out the connection between baptism and the death and resurrection of Jesus. Going down into the water and coming up again is a dying-and-rising in union with Christ (Rm 6:3-4). The implications for us are profound. As we try to live the Christian life, we discover that many self-serving instincts have to be left behind, like old clothing, if we are to experience and live new life with Christ. This is why being a Christian can seem at times to be more like dying than living. But it's only the false self – the deluded instinct, the destructive pattern – that must give way, and when it does, a new life begins. This is a pattern that repeats itself throughout the Christian life. Baptism is an end to old ways and the beginning of something new. It is about dying and rising, for the whole of our life. For Columba it included leaving his homeland permanently in order to begin monastic life.

In this context we should look at a quotation from St Paul which was taken up and developed by Blessed Columba. Speaking of Christ, Paul says, 'The death he died, he died to sin once for all; but the life he lives he lives to God. So you also must consider yourselves dead to sin and alive to God in Christ Jesus' (Rm 6:10-11). The idea of 'death to sin' and how it applies both to Christ and to us needs to be carefully examined, because the term is used in two slightly different ways. Christ himself was utterly without sin, but in his earthly life he suffered because of sin, encountered its 'attack', so to speak: he was assailed by temptation, he met with opposition, lack of faith, misunderstanding, betrayal, violence and, finally, death. But having died he was now beyond the reach of sin as manifested in this way; he was and remains, in that sense, 'dead to sin'. Our experience of sin is different: not only do we encounter it, as Christ did, outside ourselves; it is capable of being active *in* us, and we do actually sin. For us to 'die to sin' thus involves putting aside our *own* sinful ways. Baptism is a radical turning from sin and a turning towards God, but it is something that must be continually ratified and confirmed in how we think, speak and act.

Sacrament of rebirth

We can be biologically alive but dead in our relationships, even in our relationship with God. Somehow we need to come back to life. We need to be reborn. Local government authorities sometimes speak about 'urban regeneration'. Columba wants us to realise that personal regeneration is what baptism does for each of us. When water is blessed for baptism the priest prays that human nature 'may be found worthy to rise to the life of newborn children through water and the Holy Spirit'.

It is important to note that rebirth is not something we do to ourselves. Yes, we are asked to cooperate with God's action in our lives, and God will never force something without our consent, but rebirth is the work of the Holy Spirit.

Living a baptismal life

We have been given the life of Christ the Son of God for real, but we still have an older way of doing things in our system, a way which we have inherited and which needs to be dismantled. The problem is that our natural desires, all of which are fundamentally good, have been conditioned to operate in ways that are out of touch with reality. Growing into our new identity in Christ also means growing out of our old ways, and the second section of Columba's book *Christ, the*

Life of the Soul is about how to do this. Columba said, 'This Divine, God-given life is only in a state of germ. It must grow and develop in the same way as our renunciation of sin, our "death to sin" must unceasingly be renewed and sustained.'[2]

Baptism and salvation

What about the unbaptised? Columba referred to the saying 'He who believes and is baptised will be saved' (Mk 16:16), commenting that belief on its own is not enough: 'Christ adds the reception of baptism as a condition of incorporation into His kingdom'. Furthermore, Columba notes, 'all the Divine super-natural communications converge towards this sacrament or normally presuppose it'.[3] The word 'normally' here is very important, as it allows for exceptions. Important questions arise today around the salvation of those who have not been baptised. Is heaven denied to them? This is related to the question of salvation through the Church, discussed in an earlier chapter, where Columba raised the possibility of belonging to the Church through *desire*.

Similar ideas are mapped out in a broader way in the modern Catechism, which begins this topic by observing that: 'Baptism is necessary for salvation to those whom the Gospel has been proclaimed and who have had the possibility of asking for this sacrament' (CCC, 1257). It then, however, goes on to say that this is not the end of the matter:

> ⊠ Everyone who is ignorant of the Gospel of Christ and of his Church, but seeks the truth and does the will of God in accordance with his understanding of it, can be saved. It may be supposed that such persons would have *desired Baptism explicitly* if they had known its necessity. (CCC, 1260)

The Catechism holds out a similar hope for unbaptised children, based on the mercy of God and Jesus' tenderness towards children (CCC, 1261). Elsewhere Columba said, 'Christ, being God, is absolute master of His gifts and of the manner in which He distributes them; we are no more able to limit His power than we are to determine His modes of action. Christ Jesus can, when it seems good to Him, cause grace to flow directly into the soul without intermediary.'[4] Presumably this includes the grace of baptism.

   ℂ   We ought often to *thank God* from the depths of our hearts for this Divine adoption given at Baptism: it is the initial grace whence all others proceed for us. All our greatness has its source in Baptism that gave us Divine life.[5]

   ℂ   The Christian life is nothing else but the progressive and continuous development, the practical application, throughout our whole life, of this double supernatural result of 'death' and of 'life' produced by Baptism. There is all the program of Christianity.[6]

   ℂ   Our souls ought to be full of great *confidence*. In our relations with our Heavenly Father, we ought to remember we are His children though being partakers of the filiation of Christ Jesus, our Elder Brother. To doubt our adoption and the rights it gives us is to doubt Christ Himself. Let us never forget we put on Christ on the day of our Baptism: *You have put on Christ*, or rather we have been incorporated with Him. We have therefore the right to come before the Eternal Father, and say to Him: *I am Thy first-born*; to speak in the name of His Son, to ask Him with absolute confidence for all we need.[7]

NOTES

1   CLS, p. 140.

2   CLS, p. 147.

3   CLS, p. 140.

4   CLS, p. 82. These words were by way of preface to his presentation of
       the sacraments as instituted by Christ.

5   CLS, p. 150.

6   CLS, p. 148.

7   CLS, p. 150.

CHAPTER NINE

The Tragedy of Sin

℘ Sin is the real obstacle that hinders the Divine Life from developing and even from being maintained within us.[1]

Columba wrote in a letter, 'I am sixty years old to-day. The abyss of my sins and ingratitude has been swallowed up by another abyss, *infinite*, of the mercy of the Heavenly Father.'[2] The main thrust of his teaching was about the life that God wants to share with us, but this means, sooner or later, addressing the tragedy of sin, which can be understood as refusal of God's gift. In the light of God's mercy, we can have the courage to face the reality of sin, so here we examine Columba's teaching on the deadly, hellish nature of sin, and on the importance of resisting temptation.

In the parable of the Prodigal Son, a story primarily about mercy, the son leaves home, having asked for his inheritance in advance of his father's death. It is as if he has said, 'I want all that you have to offer, but I don't want you. You might as well be dead.' Sadly, this can be all too true of our way of living in the world: we want all that God has given us but we think we can do without God.[3] Sin is a refusal of God, and a refusal that Columba described in dramatic terms: 'Practically, if such a thing were not rendered impossible by the nature of the Divinity, this soul would work evil to the infinite Majesty and Goodness; it would destroy God. And was it not this that happened? When God took to Himself a human form, did not sin slay Him?'[4]

Sin is a form of death

Columba reiterated that 'God is love; love tends to unite itself with the beloved object; it requires that the beloved object should make one with itself.'[5] Sin, on the other hand, is a refusal of that relationship, a refusal of God's offer of life, a refusal, therefore, with the quality of death. We all fall short in our relationship with God in a thousand different ways, but this is different from a very deliberate choice that excludes God. Such a choice is truly deadly, and so is given the traditional term 'mortal sin'.

In his treatment of mortal sin Columba used entirely traditional terminology, speaking of 'grave matter', and of something done 'knowingly and voluntarily'.[6] The conditions that form part of this traditional description of mortal sin are very important: for something to be a mortal sin, it is not enough for a person to have done what is gravely wrong. A person has also to be *convinced* that what they are doing is gravely wrong, and, further, they must do what is wrong *with deliberate, complete consent*. Columba said mortal sin 'is a choice made with the eyes open'.[7] Teasing out what this might mean, the Catechism names factors that diminish or even remove personal culpability: unintentional ignorance (as distinct from feigned ignorance or hardness of heart), the promptings of feelings and passions, external pressures and pathological disorders (CCC, 1860). As regards the sins of others, even if we see clearly that someone has done something gravely wrong, without such full knowledge of their intentions and will as is beyond us, it is not for us to judge that they have sinned mortally. The Catechism stresses that 'we must entrust judgement of persons to the justice and mercy of God' (CCC, 1861), and I think we can take it as axiomatic that God is more just and more merciful than we are.

Columba highlighted the awfulness of sin, and its truly deadly nature, by looking to the passion of Christ: there we see the malice of sin with devastating clarity. We certainly see human sin at work in all its terrible sadness and cruelty in the sufferings of Jesus. It should alert us to what we are capable of.

Often our sin will be less than mortal. Perhaps we have done something that is gravely wrong but we were mistaken at the time or acting under pressure. Or, as happens very often, we fall short of loving God but without directly opposing God's will or friendship. The traditional name for this is *venial sin*. While the issue may not be grave, Columba points out a real danger:

    The venial faults frequently consented to without remorse, place it [the soul] in a *state* in which the supernatural action of God is constantly being thwarted. Such a soul can in no way aspire to a high degree of union with God; on the contrary, the Divine action becomes ever weaker within it; the Holy Spirit is silent; and this soul will almost infallibly fall before long into more grievous sin.[8]

A permanent refusal of God's love

Columba warned about the real possibility of hell. He saw it as the justice of God at work, ratifying and confirming the state of supernatural death freely chosen by the soul in turning away from him. Columba said at the same time:

    Far be it from me to wish to found our spiritual life upon fear of eternal punishment. For, says St. Paul, we have not received the spirit of servile fear, the spirit of the slave who dreads punishment, but the spirit of Divine adoption.[9]

The experience of hell is possible only as the result of very deliberate and persistent choices. The Catechism teaches that a wilful turning away from God is necessary, and persistence in this until the end (CCC, 1037). The pain of hell is separation from God, in whom alone we can possess the life and happiness for which we were created, and for which we long (CCC, 1035). It is a state of 'definitive self-exclusion from communion with God and the blessed' (CCC, 1033). Thus hell is something self-inflicted, despite God's insistent and continual overtures of mercy.

Overcoming temptation

In order to avoid sin, Columba proposed watchfulness, prayer and trust in Jesus Christ as our defence. Being alert to the various currents running through our mind and heart is a state of watchfulness, an important value in the monastic tradition to which Columba belonged. It's a very traditional Christian form of mindfulness. It means being alert to those ways of thinking which draw us away from treasuring our relationship with God as our true and deepest source of happiness.

Watchfulness involves an awareness of our own particular weaknesses. Some actions or situations, not so bad in themselves, can take us towards a 'point of no return' where we can resist evil with only the greatest difficulty. Chocolate lovers (of whom I am one) can find it very difficult to eat just one square of chocolate! One thing leads to another. The same dynamic can apply in situations that lead us to sin, and Columba insists we avoid such 'occasions of sin'.

Prayer above all is what strengthens us against temptation and makes clearer the dangers involved. It was as he faced temptation himself in the garden of Gethsemane that Jesus urged his disciples to watch and pray; and it was in prayer that he received consolation and light in the face of evil. Instead of praying, the disciples went to sleep, and as a result did not have the strength to stand up for Jesus in the moment of crisis. The Our Father, given to us as a model for prayer by Jesus, includes a petition for protection against temptation. St Benedict, so dear to Columba, said that temptations are to be taken in their infancy and dashed against the rock which is Christ. Prayer unites us with Christ and he is all-powerful against the evil one, triumphant over every temptation. Left to ourselves we won't stand up to temptation. With him we are able to overcome it. Prayer also reminds of us the 'taste' of what it is like to be in union with

Christ and thus makes us more aware, by contrast of the sadness and darkness that comes with sin.

  √ It might happen, through weakness, impulse or surprise, that we fall into a grave sin; but never let us say by our deeds, if not by words: 'Lord, I *know* that such a thing, however slight it may be in itself, displeases Thee, but I *will* to do it.' As soon as God asks anything of us, whatever it is, even if it should be our heart's blood, we must say: 'Yes, Lord, here I am'. If not, we shall stand still in the way of divine union, and to stand still is often to recede; it is nearly always to expose ourselves to grievous falls.[10]

  √ The habits of deliberate sin, even venial, are not formed all at once but, as you know, only little by little. 'Therefore, watch ye and pray', as Our Lord says, 'That ye enter not into temptation.'[11]

√

NOTES

1   CLS, p. 151.

2   Letter of 1 April 1918, cited in Raymond Thibaut, *Abbot Columba Marmion: A Master of the Spiritual Life 1858–1923* (London and Edinburgh: Sands & Co., 1932), p. 422.

3   Archbishop Anthony Bloom in a recorded talk, https://www.youtube.com/watch?v=uVuhaqYvKP8, accessed 24 August 2022.

4   CLS, p. 152.

5   CLS, p. 155.

6   CLS, p. 152.

7   CLS, p. 156.

8   CLS, p. 161.

9   *Christ, the Life of the Soul*, translation by Alan Bancroft (Leominster: Gracewing Publishing, 2005), p. 233.

10   CLS, p. 161.

11   CLS, p. 161.

CHAPTER TEN

The Mercy of Christ and Lifelong Repentance

80 I hear as it were a voice which says to me: 'Preach mercy!'[1]

Hearing confessions was Blessed Columba's favourite ministry when he was a diocesan priest. Later, as a monk in Belgium, he gave parish retreats, which included hearing confessions. He was obliged always to take the last train back to his abbey. He was so popular as a confessor that some people would end up finishing their confession while accompanying him to the train station, or in a corner of the lost property office. This chapter considers his teaching of the Sacrament of Penance and Reconciliation, as well as the continued process of repentance as a lifelong virtue.

Reflecting on an ancient prayer of the Mass, Columba marvelled at the fact that God manifests his 'almighty power *above all* by pardoning and showing mercy'.[2] Any consideration of repentance in our lives needs to begin with a sense of amazement at the mercy of God, and this is how Columba began his teaching on the topic.

Forgiveness based on the authority of Christ
Columba said that the basis of the Sacrament of Penance and Reconciliation is our belief in the authority of Christ to forgive sins.

He looked to the Gospel according to John, where we read that the Father has given Christ 'authority to execute judgment, because he is the Son of Man' (Jn 5:27). Furthermore, it is the idea of judgment, a judgment of infinite mercy, that dominates Columba's presentation of the sacrament. He saw the sacrament as a tribunal of mercy in which the penitent accuses himself or herself of sin before the priest, in whom Christ acts as judge. But unlike any other judge, this judge wipes away the sin of the accused and pronounces them *innocent*. The fact that the person did something wrong remains, as do the human consequences, so that the person may even have to work to repair the damage done to self and others; but the evil done is no longer a barrier between them and God. Columba quotes the prophet Isaiah in this regard: 'If your sins be as scarlet, they shall be made as white as snow' (Is 1:18).[3] Christ shares with the penitent his own justice and righteousness and restores their innocence in relation to God. The penitent's union with Christ far outweighs any kind of 'debt' of sin on their part, but they are asked to make some small gesture of repentance (called 'penance' or 'satisfaction'). In union with infinite power of Christ, their work of penance destroys sin in them and has a medicinal effect, healing them so that they can live a more holy life. The working of a normal 'courtroom' is turned on its head. In fact (and this is a very traditional idea) it may be more like a visit to the doctor.

Being contrite and confessing sin

When it comes to confessing sins, Columba wanted people to avoid becoming anxious and bogged down in minute details about what might or might not have been a sin. He saw the dangers in such a scrupulous approach to confession. He equally warned against a purely routine approach. He said that we should ask God for the gift of true contrition for our sins. Wonderfully, even the smallest trickle of imperfect contrition on our part is enough to unleash a torrent of mercy from God in the sacrament. Perhaps we don't even have any feelings of sorrow on some occasion. A lack of feeling can have so many factors that it is not to be considered in itself as a sign of a lack of contrition. Pope Francis said in an interview, 'As a confessor, even when I have found myself before a locked door, I have always tried to find a crack, just a tiny opening so that I can pry open that door and grant forgiveness and mercy.' You might not feel sorry for your sins, but it is enough even to be sorry that that is the case![4]

The prayer of absolution and the ecclesial dimension of the sacrament

Columba quoted the prayer of absolution used in his own time, in order to emphasise the redemptive work of Christ, and the fact that it is Christ who acts through the priest: '"May Jesus Christ absolve thee," says the priest, "and I, by virtue of His authority, absolve thee from thy sins."'[5] The revised version of this prayer that we use today tells the story of our reconciliation with God in richer terms, and includes the words 'Through the ministry of the Church may God give you pardon and peace.' This sacrament, like all sacraments, is the work of the whole Body of Christ, head and members. This aspect of the sacrament is more evident in communal celebrations reflecting the nature of the Church as a gathering together of people in Christ: individual confessions to a priest, absolutions and the giving of a penances are inserted into a gathering where we hear God's word together, we repent together, express our sorrow for sin together and, having received God's forgiveness, we praise God together for his mercy. The new rite also refers to this sacrament as an act of maternal care on the part of the Church. It is not just about meeting a judge or even a doctor; it is also about meeting a loving mother.

The virtue of penance

Columba wanted people to bring a spirit of repentance from the sacrament into their own daily living. Seeing it as a cultivation of an increased sensitivity to God's love with a corresponding aversion to anything that would involve turning our backs on that love, he described it as love born of forgiveness.[6]

Columba recognised that even if God has forgiven us, we still have instincts and patterns of behaviour that need to be retrained and refocussed. The Christian monastic tradition believes that the most fundamental instinct and desire of the human being is for God, with other desires and instincts ideally revolving around this, like planets around the sun. According to this view, when our desire for God is dominant, we are in our natural orbit, and it is then that we flourish.

This is where words like 'penance', 'mortification' and 'self-denial' come into play. It's not a matter of trying to kill natural inclinations that are God-given, but to realign those aspects of ourselves that are out of kilter. For Columba, mortification was not about paralysing the forces of life; it was about resisting anything opposed to life.[7] Self-denial is not self-destruction but entails refusing to let our desires for comfort and convenience dominate our way of life. The great spiritual teachers say that when our relationship with God really is planted centre stage within us, then all our other natural appetites and inclinations – far from being destroyed – are rendered all the more wonderful and beautiful.

Columba offered concrete advice about how all of this may happen in practice: keep God's commandments; follow the rules of the Church; fulfil the duties related to your state in life (for example, the duties of a parent, a spouse, an employer, an employee); work diligently; avoid situations that are likely to lead to sin. We should also become aware of our own personal besetting weaknesses through daily examination of our actions, so that we can undertake to counteract them. Perhaps a gentle daily practice would be to begin by noticing the blessings we have received from God at the end of each day, before going to notice the moments when we responded well and moments when we didn't. This situates an awareness of our weakness and tendency towards sin in the larger context of God's love.

Finally, Columba referred to the acceptance of those renunciations, reversals and losses occasioned by events permitted by divine providence. It means having a humble trust when things don't go our way, recognising that God is at work in ways that we don't perhaps understand. What God allows to happen to us can be viewed in faith as the best antidote to our own selfishness. Often it entails a kind of penance we would never have chosen for ourselves; instead, flowing from God's hand, it is far more effective. Columba suffered from eczema for many years, especially at the end of his life, but his response was characteristically good humoured. He said to the Father Infirmarian, with a laugh, 'It's my hair shirt, and so much the better that I didn't chose it for myself.' Sometimes it's not easy to distinguish between those things in life we should accept creatively and those things we should attempt to change. We can ask God for the wisdom to know the difference. As regards going further to take on voluntary penances, Columba recommended seeking the advice of a spiritual guide. This is certainly advisable regarding anything that is quite out of the ordinary.

   Contrition remains what it is, even outside the sacrament: i.e., an instrument of death to sin; but in the sacrament Christ's merits give to this instrument, as it were, infinite and supreme efficacy. It is at this moment that Christ washes our souls in His precious Blood: *Christ washed us from our sins in his own Blood* [Rv 1:5].[8]

   The more the love of God increases within us, the more we feel the need of offering to God the sacrifice of 'a contrite and humble heart': the more we feel the need of saying to Him with the publican in the Gospel: 'O God be merciful, to me a sinner.' When this feeling of compunction is habitual, it maintains the soul in great peace; it keeps it in humility: it becomes too, a powerful instrument of purification.[9]

NOTES

1   A phrase often repeated by Columba in the final years of his life.

2   This prayer is given for the Twenty-Sixth Sunday in Ordinary Time in the current Roman Missal and begins by addressing God: 'O God, who manifest your almighty power above all by pardoning and showing mercy.'

3   CLS, p. 171.

4   Pope Francis, *The Name of God is Mercy: A Conversation with Andrea Tornielli* (London: Bluebird, an imprint of Pan Macmillan, 2016), pp. 23, 31.

5   CLS, p. 170.

6   CLS, p. 173. Here Columba is quoting from Chapter XIX of Fr Frederick William Faber's book *Growth in Holiness, or, the Progress of the Spiritual Life*.

7   CLS, p. 174.

8   CLS, p. 167.

9   CLS, p. 172.

CHAPTER ELEVEN

Living the Life of Christ

> ℰ   Our activity is pleasing to God in the exact measure in which it is the overflow of our union with Him.[1]

Two decades after his death, Blessed Columba was described by one of his monks:

> ℰ   Such was Dom Marmion: a big overflowing heart; the purest and most delicate Christian charity illuminating and transfiguring every relationship; and this charity springing from the love of God, showed itself as inexhaustible as its source.[2]

This chapter explores Columba's teaching on the living out of Christian charity.

Being true to our nature
Being true to yourself is something that is highly prized these days: 'to your own self be true,' as Shakespeare put it. We must be truly human. For Columba, what distinguishes us as human beings is that we have will, reason and freedom. How we act should be governed by

our reason, which in turn should be subject to the will of God. 'He who says that he knows Him, and does not keep His commandments, is a liar and the truth is not in him' (1 Jn 2:4). Keeping God's commandments comes before adherence to any particular devotional activities towards which we might be individually drawn. Columba gave examples of how some people get it wrong:

    These people have it at heart not to miss their exercises of devotion, and this is excellent, but, for example, they do not refrain from attacking a neighbour's reputation, from telling falsehoods, and failing to keep their word; they do not scruple to give a wrong meaning to what an author has written nor to infringe the laws of literary or artistic property; they defer, sometimes to the detriment of justice, the payment of their debts, and are not exact in observing the clauses of a contract.[3]

The issues of justice and truth raised in these examples illustrate how the commandments of God are not imposed arbitrarily on us, but rather reflect the laws of our human nature. They show us the best way to live. By way of analogy we might say that a parent tells a child to stay away from the fire, not to restrict the child's freedom, but because fire can cause serious injury. God's commandments are there to enable us to flourish, and to protect us from attitudes and behaviours that would diminish our humanity.

Being true to our Christian identity

Being true to our human nature is an important part of following Christ. He is our model, and his divinity in no way diminished his humanity. As Columba said, underlining the reality of Christ's human nature, 'Christ Jesus prayed, worked, ate, suffered, slept.'[4] Similarly, our nature is neither disturbed nor lessened by God's grace, and our spiritual life involves using our own faculties – our intellect, will, affections, feelings, imagination. Furthermore, Columba proposed that we do this in a way that corresponds to the uniqueness of each person, with their own personal history, personality and God-given gifts. This reverence for personal differences permeated his spirituality. Rigid formulae, emphasis on particular devotions, rules of life, are rare in his spiritual advice. He saw an infinite delicacy in the way in which the Holy Spirit acts towards each unique person, saying that 'The splendour of a sanctity of a St Francis de Sales is not the same as that of a St Francis of Assisi; the brightness that adorns the soul of a St Gertrude or a St Teresa is quite different from that of a St Mary Magdalene.'[5] He pointed out that there are also divergences of vocations, so that, for example, long hours of prayer and meditation are not appropriate if they clash with the duties of parenthood or of obedience in religious life.

Sharing in God's own love

A major theme for Columba, as we have seen, is that Christ is our model, not only in his humanity but also in his divinity. His gift to us – through the Holy Spirit – is that we are one with him and that everything which is his is now ours, making each of us into a new creation. Living this out is the work of charity. Modern use of the word 'charity' tends to associate it with generous help to those in need. This highlights the fact that to love another is not just about rosy feelings (which may even be absent), but involves a true gift to the other. It is the opposite of being self-centred.

The theological use of the word 'charity' has, however, an even bigger meaning: it is, first and foremost, our love for God; we are drawn into the love that is eternally within the Holy Trinity. God's gift to us in Christ is a sharing in God's own love through the Holy Spirit, which has been poured into our hearts. Thus to live in charity is to refer our whole life to God, relating to God as our supreme good. This does not exclude love of neighbour but, on the contrary, gives birth to it and makes it grow.

The vine and the branches

Columba was particularly fond of the parable of the vine and the branches: we must be one with Christ as the branches are part of the vine, for 'without me you can do nothing' (Jn 15:1-5). He also recalled another organic image in the Pauline writings, where the Colossians are exhorted to live their lives 'rooted and built up' in Christ (Col 2:7). He pointed out that on some occasions we will experience this reality more vividly: there can be moments when we have an intuition of God's loving presence, a light-filled experience that touches us deeply; when faced with tasks that are tough and demanding we can be given surprising strength to see them through; when severely tempted we are enabled to remain faithful in our love of God and neighbour. Columba himself, while a young man at Holy Cross College in Dublin, experienced an intuition of God as light. The memory of this remained with him all his life. Dom Raymund Thibaut, who knew him well, described the experience:

> One day when about to re-enter the study hall after a brief absence he had all at once, without there being any outward circumstance to account for it, 'a light on God's Infinity'. … It was given to him to approach the shoreless ocean of infinite perfection and obtain a glimpse of its immensity. This light only lasted an instant, but it was so clear and strong, it penetrated so far into his mind, that he felt an imperious need to lose himself in silent adoration of the Divine Majesty. This grace …left an 'indelible impression' on his soul; it was 'as it were always present' to him, and he referred to this not without emotion and thanksgiving, during the last days of his life.[6]

When he announced the Great Jubilee of the year 2000, Pope St John Paul could have been quoting Columba. 'Everything comes from Christ, but as we belong to him, what is ours becomes his and acquires a strength that heals,'[7] he said, explaining how our actions, united to Christ, acquire eternal value like those of Christ. This could so easily have been written by Columba, in whose teaching the idea that what is ours becomes Christ's, and vice versa, is so central.

Hidden behind the ordinary in the life of a Christian who lives in Christ is something quite extraordinary, Columba believed, quoting St Thomas Aquinas: 'the perfection which results for a single soul from the gift of grace surpasses all the natural riches of the entire universe'.[8] He also referred to one of the visions of St Catherine of Siena: seeing the soul of a person for whom she had prayed, she said 'The beauty of that soul was such that no words would be able to express it'. This was, Columba observed, not a great saint in the glory of heaven, but a simple Christian, whose extraordinary beauty was given by the grace of Baptism.[9]

Not much has been said so far about love of neighbour. This is because this topic is important enough to warrant a chapter on its own. Blessed Columba's intent, at this earlier stage of the discussion, is to emphasise that charity comes as God's gift and is ultimately oriented towards God.

> To be 'True', which is the first condition necessary in order to be pleasing to God, each human action must be in conformity with our condition as free and reasonable creatures, subject to the Divine Will: otherwise this action does not correspond to our nature, to the properties belonging to it and the laws that govern it: it is false.[10]

> Baptism has grafted us onto Christ, and henceforth has have the Divine sap of His grace in us. It is thus that we can accomplish all our actions divinely, because the inward principle is Divine. And when this principle is so powerful that it becomes the only one, and our whole activity springs from it, then we fulfil the words of St Paul: 'I live', that is to say, I exercise my human and personal activity; 'now, not I but Christ liveth in me': it is Christ Who lives, because the principle on which all my own activity, all my personal life is based, is the grace of Christ.[11]

ഇ

NOTES

1   Letter of 2 November 1915, quoted in Dom Raymond Thibaut, *Abbot Columba Marmion: A Master of the Spiritual Life 1858–1923* (London and Edinburgh, Sands & Co., 1932), p. 348.

2   Dom Raymond Thibaut, *Abbot Columba Marmion: A Master of the Spiritual Life 1858–1923* (London and Edinburgh, Sands & Co., 1932), p. 404.

3   CLS, p. 184.

4   CLS, p. 185.

5   CLS, p. 190.

6   Dom Raymond Thibaut, *Abbot Columba Marmion: A Master of the Spiritual Life 1858–1923* (London and Edinburgh, Sands & Co., 1932), p. 20.

7   Bull of Call for the Great Jubilee Of the Year 2000, *Incarnationis mysterium*, 10, https://www.vatican.va/jubilee_2000/docs/documents/hf_jp-ii_doc_30111998_bolla-jubilee_sp.html, accessed 13 September 2022.

8   *Summa Theologica*, I–II, q. CXIII, a. 9, ad 2, quoted in CLS, p. 191.

9   From the *Life of St Catherine* by Blessed Raymond of Capua, quoted in CLS, p. 191.

10   CLS, p. 183.

11   CLS, p. 191.

Our Growth in Christ

  With all the energy of our being, by the meritorious practice of the virtues, above all, the theological virtues, and by the essential disposition of doing all for the glory of the Heavenly Father, let us aim at leaving the greatest freedom possible to the development within us of the action of God and of the Holy Spirit.[1]

On the eve of his profession as a monk, Columba wrote in his personal notebook, 'I resolved to try to imitate this perfect offering [of Christ] by making my profession a holocaust of faith, hope and charity.'[2] This chapter looks at Columba's teaching on how we grow in these and other virtues, complementing his thoughts with some ideas from today's Catechism.

Acquired virtues: growing in moral strength

Columba used the analogy of learning a language to explain the idea of an acquired virtue. After much repetition and practice, a person acquires a habitual ability to handle a language and understand it in a way that has something stable about it. They have acquired a certain strength (*virtus* in Latin) which they didn't have before.

Something similar also happens in the moral life: through repeated courageous acts we acquire the virtue of courage; by expressing ourselves sincerely many times, we acquire the virtue of sincerity, and so on. Through these virtues, the acts of courage and sincerity of expression become easier and more natural to us. God has made us in such a way that we can grow in moral strength.

Among the acquired moral virtues, Columba included examples such as courage, strength, prudence, justice, gentleness, loyalty and sincerity, and there are more. The wide range of moral virtues is traditionally summarised and reduced to four 'cardinal' virtues: prudence, fortitude, justice and temperance. All the many moral virtues 'refer to or are implied by' these fundamental virtues.[3]

Prudence is the ability to make good moral decisions in each concrete situation, to see what must be done, even if it is difficult or dangerous. The virtue of justice enables us to be consistently firm in our resolve to give what is due to both God and neighbour. It respects the rights of others. Temperance enables us to be wise and moderate in following our desires. For example, when it comes to eating, it means we will eat enough to be healthy but not so much as to be harmful. Fortitude is the ability to remain firm and constant, especially when being morally good turns out to be demanding; it's a kind of moral 'grit' that includes courage when we are afraid to do what is truly good. All such human virtues are acquired by education, by deliberate acts and by perseverance, and are renewed by repeated efforts.

From the Catechism: human virtues and God's grace[4]

The Catechism tells us that the goal of the virtuous life is to become like God and to live in union with God. The efforts we make to be just, true courageous and balanced in our moral living strengthen our orientation towards all that is good, and ultimately towards God. And yet anyone with an ounce of self-knowledge knows that, left to our own devices, we fail morally all the time. We need God's help, which is given to us when we ask for it. God purifies our motives and intentions, and helps to train our sights on what is best. The moral virtues we acquire through our own effort are already an opening to God and happen only with God's help. God gives us light and strength when we ask for it. Finally:

ଓ   The human virtues are rooted in the theological virtues, which adapt man's faculties for participation in the divine nature:[5] for the theological virtues relate directly to God. They dispose Christians to live in a relationship with the Holy Trinity. They have the One and Triune God for their origin, motive, and object. (CCC, 1812)

And so, as Columba taught, our growth in virtue involves a constant interplay between God's grace and our effort.

The theological virtues of faith, hope and love

Faith, hope and love are called 'theological virtues' because they directly concern our relationship with God. They are also called 'infused virtues' because they come as a gift directly from God, and not as the result of our own effort. Columba has reiterated all along that the Christian life is a sharing in the identity of Christ, human and divine. We could say that the theological virtues are the strengths with which we live 'divinely'. God can help us to act in ways that exceed our level of natural virtue. Some members of Alcoholics Anonymous have experienced this.

Faith is the first of these virtues, says Columba, since we are all called to know God, and this happens through faith because we do not yet see God face to face: we know God through the revelation of Jesus Christ.

ଓ   This knowledge of faith is then a Divine knowledge, and that is why Our Lord said it is a knowledge that gains eternal life. *Now this is eternal life: that they MAY KNOW Thee, the only true God, and Jesus Christ Whom Thou has sent* [Jn 17:3].[6]

One example of this would be St Peter's intuition about the true identity of Jesus. Jesus had asked the disciples who people thought he was. After they gave a variety of answers, he then asked them, 'Who do you say that I am?' It was Peter who spoke up, saying 'You are the Messiah, the Son of the living God.' Jesus said 'Flesh and blood has not revealed this to you, but my Father in heaven'. In other words, this knowledge was of divine, not human origin (Mt 16:17).

Knowledge of God through faith gives birth to hope:

> ℅ In this light of faith we know where our beatitude lies; we know that which 'eye hath not seen nor ear heard, neither hath it entered into the heart of man to conceive', that is to say, the beauty and greatness of the glory that 'God hath prepared for them who love him' [1 Cor 2:9].[7]

This happiness is beyond what we can achieve of our own nature, but hope assures us that this gift will be ours.

And, finally charity, of which Columba said, 'It makes us experience a real complacency in God; we prefer God to all things and we seek to manifest towards Him this taking of complacency and this preference by observing His will.'[8] It colours the other virtues with an explicit love of God.

The more we allow our lives to be animated by faith, hope and love, the more God increases these gifts within us, according to Columba. Furthermore, he said that living by the acquired virtues of prudence, fortitude, justice and temperance helps to protect the gifts that God has given.

Columba saw more value in all the small things that are done in love, than in big, dramatic works that are weak in love.[9] On one occasion an elderly sister in a convent to which he was a regular visitor had heard that he was travelling to stay for some time in a Benedictine convent in Scotland. Thinking it was a huge distance away, she wondered if he might bring back a flower from that distant land. He got wind of this and, when he finally arrive back, brought a marigold, all crumpled up, in a little enveloped addressed to the sister in question.

Columba pointed out that Jesus' life was, in outward appearance, so ordinary that his neighbours were scandalised when he began to preach the word of God to them. And yet, he stressed, every action of Jesus was of infinite value to the Father, for two reasons: firstly, it was an action of the Son of God; secondly, everything he did was for the love of the Father. Columba said that we can really imitate this twofold perfection. By God's gift, we are sons and daughters of God along with Jesus, sharing his identity; secondly we can cultivate an attitude whereby our actions become increasingly animated by love of God. In this way the perfection of Christ's life can be mirrored in ours. A friend whose family Columba visited regularly remembered how much they enjoyed his visits adding that 'In the midst of the conversation and the sallies of his wit, all at once a remark, a single word, a simple gesture, such as that of raising his eyes to heaven, made the 'man' suddenly give place to the servant of God. But this was done so naturally, without a shadow of affectation, it rose so spontaneously from the depth of his soul, that the contrast was simply delightful.'[10]

Referring all our actions to God

Columba suggests continual renewal of the intentions by which we act. It is not possible for us to be explicitly aware at every moment of an intention to act for the love of God, but we can stop every now and then and make an explicit act of self-dedication to God in what we do. We don't need complicated formulas of words to refer what we do to God: 'a single glance of the heart can contain an intensity of love'.[11]

> ℬ Supernatural charity is a pearl of great price, an inestimable treasure, but it is exposed to be lost by any grave fault whatsoever. That is why it is necessary to protect it on all sides; and such is the function of the *moral virtues*. These virtues are the safeguards of love.[12]

so A pure intention frequently renewed, surrenders the soul to God in its being and in its activity; it unceasingly reanimates and maintains in the soul the fire of Divine love; and thus by each good work it causes to be done and referred to God, it increases the life of the soul.[13]

so

NOTES

1   CLS, p. 212.

2   From his personal spiritual notes, 9 February 1891, cited in in Raymond Thibaut, *Abbot Columba Marmion: A Master of the Spiritual Life 1858-1923* (London and Edinburgh: Sands & Co., 1932), p. 80.

3   CLS, p. 201.

4   Columba also spoke about infused moral virtues which come, not as a result of our effort, but directly as God's gift, but the picture he presents is very complex, and there is a history of theological dispute about this idea, such that a full discussion of it would require a lot of space. This is why I think it is better to look to the simpler approach of the Catechism, which, significantly, does not refer to infused moral virtues, but does not contradict this idea either.

5   The Catechism includes the footnote: Cf. 2 Pet 1:4.

6   CLS, p. 196.

7   CLS, p. 196.

8   CLS, p. 197. The word 'complacency' is used here in a way that is perhaps unfamiliar to contemporary readers. 'Complacency in God' means experiencing pleasure in God.

9   CLS, p. 199.

10   Raymond Thibaut, *Abbot Columba Marmion: A Master of the Spiritual Life 1858–1923* (London and Edinburgh: Sands & Co., 1932), p. 407.

11   CLS, p. 207.

12   CLS, p. 201.

13   CLS, p. 205.

The Eucharistic Sacrifice of Christ

℥   Our Lord wished to institute this Sacrament at the moment when, by His Passion, He was about to give us the greatest testimony perpetuated among us 'in commemoration of him'. It is like His last thought for us and the testament of His Sacred Heart: *this do for the commemoration of me*.[1]

Blessed Columba saw the Eucharistic Sacrifice as the centre and sun around which his life as a priest revolved, something beyond human words. Each afternoon, praying before the Blessed Sacrament, he offered everything he was doing that day as a preparation for the offering of Mass the following morning. He did in fact try to put something of the reality of the Eucharist into words, and there's much to be gained from exploring and grappling with his ideas, especially in light of recent developments in Eucharistic theology, and the synthesis given in the Catechism.

The sacrifice of Christ
Columba began his treatment of the sacrifice of the Mass by considering Christ as priest, as mediator between humanity and

God. The priests of the Old Testament offered sacrifices, and these foreshadowed the sacrifice that Christ was to offer, namely himself. Before considering this in more detail, Columba considered the meaning of religious sacrifice in general.

He saw sacrifice as an expression of our relationship with God: absolute adoration. Columba said that supreme homage would have to go as far as self-annihilation, except that God does not allow us to sacrifice our own lives in this way. Instead, human beings take things that serve their existence, such as bread, fruit, animals etc., and destroy these instead. Annihilation is however only one way of looking at sacrifice, and maybe not the best. The Old Testament in fact ascribed a variety of meanings to sacrificial offerings. Some biblical scholars see a completely different overarching theme in these sacrifices: they all use food, and sacrifice can be seen as a way of sharing food with God, the closest we can get to having a meal with God. This is far from annihilation.

Columba placed special emphasis on the annual Jewish sacrifice of atonement in which the victim was substituted for the people. It was killed in place of them because they deserved death for their sins, and its death brought them forgiveness.

But this is not an accurate reading of the Old Testament texts, the details of which would make this chapter far too long. Suffice it to say by way of example that there were two animals involved in the ritual, and the one that carried the sins of the people was not killed but sent off into the desert. While the New Testament Letter to the Hebrews does draw a parallel between the rite of atonement performed by the high priest in the temple sanctuary, and the entry of Christ the true High Priest into the sanctuary of heaven, the connections and allusions are more complex and more subtle. Particularly to be avoided, I think, is the idea that the 'death-blow' that Jesus suffered came from God the Father (an idea that Columba actually suggested); this is nowhere in the New Testament.

As an alternative view, we can look to St Augustine's theology of sacrifice, where the core of sacrifice is union with God, not annihilation. The word 'sacrifice' has its roots in two Latin words:

sacrum facere – to make holy, to set apart for God. For Augustine anything we do that unites us or others more closely to God is a sacrifice. The true purpose of sacrifice is 'clinging to God and helping our neighbour to the same end'.[2] This shows the sacrifice of Christ in a very different light: it is the ultimate example of an act of union with God, or anything done to help others towards union with God. This was the story of his whole life, death and resurrection. St Augustine's idea of sacrifice as union also fits very well with the notion of sacrifice as a 'meal with God', since meals together are all about sharing life in a very tangible way.

Eucharist: memorial of Christ's saving deeds

Columba called the altar a 'new Calvary',[3] basing his theology of the sacrifice of the Mass on some oft-quoted texts from the Council of Trent: for example, the Mass as a true sacrifice that 'recalls and renews Christ's immolation on Calvary'.[4] After Vatican II, the Catechism broadened the picture, recovering other important aspects of the Mass's meaning that had received less attention in recent centuries.

While the Catechism says that the sacrifice of Christ, offered once for all on the Cross, is present in the Eucharist (CCC, 1353), it also broadens the scope to say that the Eucharist is a memorial of his life, death and resurrection and his continual intercession for us before the Father (CCC, 1337, 1340, 1341). The Eucharistic prayers used at Mass refer explicitly to the fact that the Eucharist is a memorial of this kind. Most of them also include Christ's ascension in the memorial, joined to an anticipation of his return in glory. The implication is that in the Eucharist we are put into real contact with the life, death, resurrection, ascension, and heavenly intercession of Christ, in a real anticipation of his return in glory.

It is particularly important to understand that 'memorial' in this context means more than the idea that those present think about what happened long ago, a purely psychological remembering. 'In the liturgical celebration of these events, they become in a certain way present and real' (CCC, 1363). This making present of what happened 'once for all' is the work of the Holy Spirit (CCC, 1104).

As with the theology of the cross that I proposed in an earlier chapter, the sacrificial memorial of the Mass presented in these texts is an entry into the full sweep of all that Christ has done for us in his life, death and resurrection, seen as a single event of self-sacrificing love for us, and loving obedience to the Father. This is a broader version of sacrifice than Columba's.

Body and blood of Christ

The Eucharist is consecrated under two signs, and Columba saw here a mystical sign of Christ's death: the idea here is that presence of Christ's body and blood under *separate* signs is a sign of the *separation* of his body and blood on the cross, in other words, his death. This is a relatively new idea in the history of theology and was popular in Columba's time. Yet it is interesting to note that neither the Constitution on the Liturgy of Vatican II nor the Catechism take up this line of thought, preferring to rely largely on biblical texts to bring out the connection between the Mass and the sacrifice of Christ.

While the words 'body' and 'blood' are used to refer to the two separate species of the Eucharist, Catholic tradition holds that Christ is fully and completely present under each sign. Thus, to put it crudely but not without reverence, 'body' and 'blood' as received in the Eucharist cannot refer to physical 'parts' of the humanity of Christ distinctly present, but to Christ, whole and entire, yet experienced in two different ways. Each sign points to his presence and the meaning of his self-sacrificing love in a different way. By way of example, the *General Instruction of the Roman Missal*, when it encourages reception from the chalice, says,

 ℠ For in this form the sign of the Eucharistic banquet is more clearly evident and clear expression is given to the divine will by which the new and eternal Covenant is ratified in the Blood of the Lord, as also the relationship between the Eucharistic banquet and the eschatological banquet in the Father's Kingdom. (GIRM, 281)

Each sign thus makes certain things *more evident* and gives them *clearer expression*. On this basis we can say, as a minimum, the presence of Christ under the sign of wine points to the new covenant in his blood (an unbreakable bond uniting us with God through Christ), to the festive banquet of the Eucharist, and to the heavenly banquet of which it is a foretaste. The presence of Christ under the sign of bread shows him to be our Manna, our Bread from Heaven, and we are one body through sharing in one loaf. The use of bread and wine also shows Christ to be an eternal priest prefigured by Melchisedek, who brought bread and wine (Gn 14:18). We can begin to see that when Jesus instituted this sacrament under two signs its meaning was very rich indeed, and here we have touched only on some aspects.

A whole book could be written about the significance of these two signs. Not only do they refer to Christ present to us in sacrament, but also to what he has done for us in his life, death and resurrection. The Eucharist is like the appearance of the risen Christ in the upper room, showing his wounds to his disciples (Jn 20:20), showing his body *given up* for us, and his blood *poured out* for us: the *event* of his death and resurrection is present here and now. This is a simple biblical image of the Mass as a sacramental memorial, and I think Columba would have approved of it as a summary of the core of his teaching on the sacrifice of the Mass.

The richness of Christ's gift to us in the Eucharist
Having unfolded for the reader the sacrificial nature of the Mass, Columba drew out some of the implications for those who worship. Even if I have questioned and developed some aspects of his interpretation of the Eucharistic sacrifice, the implications which he enumerated still stand as important pointers for worship today.

Christ in his life, death and resurrection, gives *infinite homage* to the Father. This infinite homage is present and active in the Mass so that we can be drawn into it and be united with it. Our worship gives true glory to God because it is done 'through him, with him and in him.'

The words of Jesus used in the Eucharistic prayers speak of the blood of the new and eternal covenant, poured out 'for the forgiveness of sins'. The Mass is, according to Columba, a source of *confidence and pardon*. In the Eucharist we encounter the 'Lamb of God who takes away the sins of the world'.

Columba pointed to the Eucharist as the ultimate act of *thanksgiving*. The Greek word *eucharistein* means in fact 'to give thanks'. In the Eucharistic prayers of the Mass we recall that Jesus blessed the bread and wine, giving thanks to the Father. In the Mass we continue to do what Jesus did, and so the Eucharistic prayer of blessing over the bread and wine is a great act of thanksgiving.

Columba also spoke about the Eucharist as *petition or supplication*. Taking the lead from the Letter to the Hebrews (7:25), he would have us 'approach the throne of grace' in the Mass above all 'with confidence' to find grace when we are in the need of help. He said that there is no grace that we cannot ask for and obtain.

Columba pointed out that the offering of the Mass involved all the faithful, not just the priest: when the priest invites people to pray he refers to 'my sacrifice and yours'. He also quoted the Roman Canon (now the First Eucharist Prayer in the Roman Missal), which says that *all present* at Mass offer a sacrifice of praise to God and further, that this offering is of God's *whole family*. For Columba, another sign of this was the presentation of the bread, wine and other gifts by the faithful, an ancient ritual that had disappeared, but was thankfully restored after Vatican II. He was ahead of his time in rediscovering its importance.

Columba developed the idea of our *union* with Christ in the Eucharist, reflecting on how bread and wine are produced: many grains are brought together to make one loaf,[5] and many grapes are crushed to form but one liquid. In Christ we are one. He also quoted the prayer said by the priest when he mingles water and wine: 'Through the mystery of this water and wine, may we come to share in the divinity of Christ, who humbled himself to share in our humanity.' The water and wine are so mingled as to become one, and so it is with us and Christ.

∞ I see plainly that if I could make my life a perpetual preparation and thanksgiving for Holy Mass, that I would receive the most extraordinary graces.[6]

∞ Everything comes to us from our Father in heaven, through Christ Jesus in Whom God has placed all the treasures of holiness that men can desire; this Jesus is there upon the altar with His treasures, not only present, but offering Himself for us to the glory of His Father, rendering Him, at this moment, the most perfect homage He can desire, renewing the sacrifice of the cross, to as to continue it and apply its supreme efficacy to us. If we have a profound conviction of these truths there is no grace we cannot ask and obtain.[7]

∞

NOTES

1   CLS, p. 215.

2   Augustine, *De Civitate Dei*, X, cc. 5–6.

3   CLS, p. 220.

4   Council of Trent, Session XII, canon 1. Quoted in translation in CLS, p. 215.

5   This image is very old indeed, found in the *Didache or Teaching of the Apostles*, which dates from the end of the first century.

6   Personal notes written on the Feast of the Sacred Heart, 1888. Given in Raymond Thibaut, *Abbot Columba Marmion: A Master of the Spiritual Life 1858–1923* (London & Edinburgh: Sands & Co., 1932), p. 76.

7   CLS, p. 224.

CHAPTER FOURTEEN

Christ the Bread of Life

   ॐ When we assimilate the food of the body, we change it into our own substance, while Christ gave Himself to us as food in order to transform us into Himself.[1]

When Blessed Columba spoke to his monks about the Eucharist, he did so in two separate talks, which appeared later as two distinct chapters in *Christ, the Life of the Soul*: 'The Eucharistic Sacrifice' and 'The Bread of Life'. There are historical roots to this way of looking at the topic, especially the influence of the Council of Trent (1545–63), which shaped the theology, spirituality and pastoral practice of the Catholic Church for four hundred years. This council did not set out to provide a complete presentation of Eucharistic theology, but to respond to Protestant criticisms.

Among the teachings that sixteenth-century Protestants called into question were the Catholic idea of the sacrifice of the Mass and the Catholic teaching about the presence of Christ in the Eucharist. The council answered these questions as separate issues, with one result being that Catholic pastoral teaching after the council tended to present these perspectives on the Eucharist separately. But they really belong together. Christ present in the Eucharist is Christ who has offered himself for us, once and for all; and the most profound way to enter into the sacrifice of Christ is by Holy Communion. The reform of the liturgy after Vatican II retained the theology of the sacrifice of Christ in the Mass,[2] but it made it clearer that this sacrifice becomes present in the form of a meal. This is simply and beautifully expressed in the acclamation after the consecration: 'When we eat this Bread and drink this Cup, we proclaim your Death, O Lord, until you come again'. 'Meal' and 'sacrifice' should not be pitted against one another in discussion of the Eucharist since the theological reality of the sacrifice becomes present in the form of a meal. If this had been clearer around the time of the Protestant Reformation, much of the polemics that endured for centuries might have been avoided. The 'Eucharistic Sacrifice' and the 'Bread of Life' really belong together as they are describing the same reality, albeit from two separate vantage points.

The keynote of Columba's second chapter on the Eucharist comes from chapter six of the Gospel according to John, where Jesus refers to himself as the 'bread of life', saying 'Whoever eats me lives by my life' (Jn 6:57). Building on this, Columba said that 'He is life by nature; whosoever eats Him eats Life.'[3] Focusing on Jesus' teaching that whoever eats his flesh and drinks his blood 'abides in me and I in him' (Jn 6:56), he emphasised the importance of union with Christ through the Eucharist. For Columba this meant being one with Christ firstly by being, with him, a child of God. Here again is Columba's great theme: divine adoption. But Columba went further. Abiding in Christ means also believing in him. It means submitting our will to him. Columba boldly asserted that through our 'abiding in him' a union is established between us and Christ that is analogous to the unity between Jesus' own humanity and his divinity.[4] In all of this, Christ is to be the mainspring of all our interior activity.

℘ When the soul remains given up to Him, to His every will, then Christ's action becomes so powerful that this soul will infallibly be carried on to the highest perfection, according to God's designs. For Christ comes to the soul with His Divinity, His merits, His riches, to be its Light and Way, its Truth, Wisdom, Justice and Redemption: *Who of God is made unto us wisdom, and justice, and sanctification, and redemption* [1 Cor 1:30], in a word, to be the Life of the soul, to live Himself within the soul: *I live, now not I; but Christ liveth in me* [Gal 2:20].[5]

Reflecting on the bread of life as food, Columba took up a theme that echoes down the centuries of Church tradition: when we eat ordinary food what we eat becomes part of us, assimilated into us, whereas in the Eucharist *we are transformed into what we eat*. This section of his teaching is a tissue of quotations, showing the degree to which he had imbibed the ideas of Church fathers and theologians.

It was in fact a return to the great sources of Christian tradition in a way that would come to be known as *ressourcement*, and would go on to inform and shape the later theological renewal of Vatican II. Columba cites, for example, the fifth-century Church Fathers Pope St Leo the Great and St Augustine of Hippo on the subject. 'Participation in the body and blood of Christ,' he quotes Leo as saying, 'produces in us none other effect than to make us pass into what we take.'[6] Driving this point home, he quotes Augustine's account some decades earlier of a vision of Christ saying to him: 'I am the nourishment of the strong; have faith and eat me. But you will not change me into yourself; it is you who will be transformed into me.'[7] Having drawn on two of the greatest thinkers of the Church's first centuries, he turns then to St Thomas Aquinas, who wrote roughly halfway between their day and his own and who he believes expresses the reality is a characteristically clear way: 'But the Eucharistic nourishment, instead of being transformed into the one who takes it, transforms that person into Itself.'[8] Thomas, he says, develops the idea of our union with Christ even further by emphasising how our love of Christ should enable our reception of Eucharist to bear fruit as love. 'The efficacy of this sacrament is to work a certain transformation into Christ by means of charity,' Columba quotes him as saying, continuing: 'And that is its distinctive fruit … The property of charity is to transform him who loves into the object of his love.'[9] Taken together, these ideas hammer home the fact that, if the sacrificial presence of Christ in Holy Communion is wonderful, in the end its only purpose is to transform us. Its purpose is in fact just as wonderful: that we are transformed into Christ himself. We become what we receive, if we cooperate with Christ's love.

Preparation for Holy Communion and thanksgiving

In view of the immense gift given to us in the Eucharist, Columba would have us prepare properly for it. By way of remote preparation we should frequently renew a total gift of ourselves to Christ and disengage from anything that prevents such a gift of self to him. This means looking at bad habits and lack of generosity. It means looking at our relationships with others and being reconciled with our neighbour. Coldness towards others or resentment have no place here. Union with Christ is union with the 'whole Christ', that is with Christ the head, and those who are members of his body. He writes, 'When Our Lord finds a soul thus disposed, given up entirely and unreservedly to His action, He acts in it with His Divine virtue which works marvels of holiness because it meets with no obstacle.'[10] Columba also advised that all our actions be done with a view to our next participation in the Eucharist, offering all we do to God through Christ. A visit to the Blessed Sacrament each day is a good time to include an act by which we offer everything to God in preparation for Mass.

Columba wrote at a time when people would engage in various devotions during Mass, since the words of the prayers and readings were largely inaccessible to them. The prayers were, after all, in Latin, and many of them were only whispered by the priest. People wanted to unite themselves with what was happening during the Mass but, since the Middle Ages, would have had to find some way of praying during Mass. Some people prayed the rosary, for example, while others meditated on the life of Christ or recited other prayers as the liturgy progressed.

Columba was not a liturgical reformer, and simply suggested solutions for the liturgical experience as he found it. He suggested that each person find that particular preparation during Mass which most suited them personally; but he made special reference to the prayers of the Mass, which would have been available in translation, as a good basis for preparation. The liturgical movement had begun to realise that the liturgical prayers and readings themselves were the ideal source of Christian spirituality and, in the early twentieth century, missals for lay people were published for the first time with the Latin and the vernacular texts printed side by side. For Columba, the best possible preparation for Holy Communion was to follow the actual prayers and rites of the Mass rather than focusing on something else, no matter how sublime. Here we see an instinct that found full expression after Vatican II, when the liturgy is celebrated in the language of the people. Thus the Council would later say, 'Mother Church earnestly desires that all the faithful should be led to that fully conscious, and active participation in liturgical celebrations which is demanded by the very nature of the liturgy.'[11]

Thanksgiving after Holy Communion is another area where Columba envisaged a wide freedom, so that each person would find their own best way of doing this. This is typical of his approach to spiritual teaching as a whole: his main concern was to present the reader with a broad outline of how God works with us, without trying to impose any particular devotional approach but rather respecting the fact that God works in different ways with different people according to their needs. In his day people continued to pray quietly after receiving Holy Communion, while the priest purified the vessels and concluded Mass. Some also continued with prayers of thanksgiving after Mass was over. The liturgy as we find it today incorporates thanksgiving for everyone together into the Communion Rite, either by a communal hymn of thanksgiving, or a time of silent prayer. This need not prevent some later moment of thanksgiving outside the liturgy.

Back to divine adoption

For Columba, 'To receive Christ is to make a statement of faith of the largest kind, and consequently it is to share in the highest possible measure in the Divine Sonship of Christ.'[12] The core of Columba's spiritual teaching as a whole is, as we have seen, our divine adoption. According to him, Eucharistic Communion is 'the most perfect act of our Divine adoption'.[13] The idea of sharing in the divine nature through Christ is so staggering that it is hard for us to take in; perhaps more amazing is the thought that such a simple gesture as sharing in Holy Communion could bring this about.

ৰ There is no action wherein our faith can be exercised with greater intensity than in Communion; there is no more sublime homage of faith than to believe in Christ whose Divinity and Humanity are both hidden under the appearances of the Host.[14]

ৰ Why should not the faithful use the same prayers that our Holy Mother the Church puts on the lips of the priest to prepare him to receive our Lord? In thus preparing ourselves, we are united more directly to the Sacrifice of Christ and to the intentions of His Sacred Heart.[15]

ৰ Our Lord is with His Mystical Body; all Christians are His members by grace, and when we communicate we must do so with the whole Christ, that is to say, unite ourselves by charity with Christ in his physical being and with His members; we cannot separate the two. This is why the least wilful coldness, the least resentment harboured in the soul towards our neighbour form a great obstacle to the perfection of that union which Our Lord wishes to have with us in the Eucharist.[16]

సం

NOTES

1   CLS, p. 233.

2   For example the new Eucharistic prayers speak of 'this holy and living sacrifice', 'oblation', 'sacrificial Victim' (Third Eucharistic Prayer) 'Sacrifice', 'living sacrifice' and 'offering' (Fourth Eucharistic Prayer).

3   CLS, p. 231.

4   CLS, p. 233.

5   CLS, p. 233.

6   Sermon 63 on the Passion, 12, c. 7.

7   *Confessions*, VII, c. 10.

8   *In IV Senten.*, dist. 12, q.2, a.1.

9   CLS, p. 234.

10   CLS, p. 239.

11   *Sacrosanctum concilium*, 14.

12   *Christ, the Life of the Soul*, translation by Alan Bancroft (Leominster: Gracewing Publications: 2005), p. 383. Note: This sentence is missing from the translation used elsewhere in this book.

13   CLS, p. 243.

14   CLS, p. 243.

15   CLS, p. 244.

16   CLS, p. 238.

The Prayer of Christ and his Church

     ⅋   I find great devotion when reciting the *Gloria Patri*[1] in uniting with the Adorable Trinity in that eternal hymn of praise which It is ever offering to Itself with infinite love, and (in uniting) with the whole court of heaven.[2]

A glance through the personal notes of Blessed Columba shows that many of his most profound insights came from meditating on the liturgical prayers of the Church, as well as the scripture readings and other texts used throughout the liturgical year. An appreciation of the liturgical year was so important to Columba that he devoted an entire book to it, *Christ in His Mysteries*. Here we will examine his teaching on the public prayer of the Church and the liturgical year, beginning with Christ himself and then looking at the Church's share in Christ's prayer.

The infinite canticle in the life of the Trinity
Columba said that even if God had never created the world, there would still be a never-ending hymn of divine praise. He reminded his readers that God is triune (one God in three persons, three persons in one God) and that within the Trinity itself 'the Father contemplates

his Word; He sees in Him the perfect, substantial, living image of Himself; such is the essential glory that the Father receives'. The second person of the Blessed Trinity is 'a Divine canticle, a living canticle, singing the praise of the Father, expressing the plenitude of his perfections'.[3] This 'infinite hymn which resounds unceasingly in the bosom of the Father' took flesh and became human in Jesus. On the lips of Jesus, this hymn of praise took on a human expression and human accents. Furthermore, Jesus has united all of humanity with himself so that his praise, his prayer, his petition become ours. The Church is the body of Christ and shares in his adoration of the Father. This is why our prayer is 'through Christ our Lord'.

The prayer of the Church

We have already seen how Columba looked at the union between the Church and Christ in the Eucharist. He saw the Eucharist as the centre of the Church's larger cycle of daily prayer, also called the *Liturgy of the Hours* or *The Divine Office*. In Columba's time this prayer was prayed almost exclusively by priests and religious. The Benedictine Office which Columba followed had seven different Offices of daily prayer and one during the night (normally very early morning, before dawn). Some of them, such as Terce, Sext and None, lasted not much more than ten minutes, while Lauds and Vespers could be about a half hour in length. The 'night' office celebrated in the very early morning was the longest. The Roman office as prayed by priests in parishes was also demanding and was adjusted after Vatican II so that it would be less burdensome and more spiritually nourishing, and further adaptations were introduced with the hope that at least some of the offices might be prayed by lay people as well. The daily office of large churches in the early centuries of the Church was such that lay people could take part with ease at major moments such as morning prayer and evening prayer but it became increasingly elaborate and beyond the scope of what could be done in an ordinary parish. Since Vatican II it has been readapted and promoted once again as a prayer for everyone in the Church. This is particularly important in places where daily Mass is not possible; the

Liturgy of the Hours is a true sharing in the prayer of Christ himself. It is the original daily liturgy of the Church and predates daily Mass. Pastoral resources are now being published to enable lay people to lead these liturgies with ease, and this form of daily prayer is gaining popularity both for groups in parishes and for individual use.

A particular strength of this prayer is that it is divinely inspired since, as Columba pointed out, most of it is from the scriptures, especially the psalms. He said, 'Read the Divine pages. You will see how these canticles, inspired by the Holy Ghost, *relate, proclaim and exalt the perfections of God*.'[4] The psalms also express human feelings and needs. The whole of human life is there, good, bad and ugly. 'The psalms,' he observes, 'know how to weep and rejoice; to desire and supplicate.'[5]

The psalms also speak of Christ, and this was particularly important for Columba. Biblical scholarship shows that the Book of Psalms is quoted more often in the New Testament than any other Old Testament book. In Luke 24:44 we read, 'Everything written about me in the law of Moses, the Prophets *and the Psalms*, must be fulfilled.' Think of 'My God, my God, why have you forsaken me?' (Ps 22) or 'The stone which the builders rejected has become the cornerstone' (Ps 118, also quoted by Jesus about himself). The face of Christ at prayer emerges vividly in some lines of the psalms, and the gospels also show Jesus praying using words from the psalms.

The prayer of the bride and the bridegroom

Columba was very fond of the image of the 'bride leaning on her Beloved' found in the Old Testament love poetry of the *Song of Songs*. Following a tradition that was centuries old, he saw it was an image of the Church, and of each of us individually. The Divine Office is 'the voice of the Bride, the voice that delights the Bridegroom. It is the canticle sung by the Church in company with Christ' and 'in God's sight it surpasses in value all our private prayers'.[6] The power of the Church's prayer comes from her union with Christ; this is what Columba meant by 'leaning on her Beloved'.

The mysteries of Christ in the liturgical year

The liturgical year celebrates the great events of Christ: his incarnation, life, death, resurrection, ascension and sending of the Holy Spirit. Columba called these the 'mysteries of Christ' that the Church unfolds for her children during the year. He pointed out that the liturgical year doesn't just draw on the particular gospel passage for each mystery, but goes deeper by looking to all the other books of the Bible to 'penetrate into the very sentiments that animated the Heart of Jesus'. [7] This is a very traditional way of approaching the Bible, one where the deepest meaning of each passage is found by reading it in the light of other texts throughout the scriptures, Old Testament and New.

The mysteries of Christ are not just something from the past. Columba described them as 'living mysteries'. According to him, Christ's mysteries are now ours. He quoted, as an example the words of St Leo the Great: 'In adoring our Saviour's birth, it follows that it is our own origin we celebrate … and the birth of the Head is at the same time the birth of His mystical body.'[8] When we enter into the seasons of Lent and Easter with faith, this brings about a 'death to sin' in us, and a grace of spiritual life and liberty.

Even the celebrations of the saints are, according to Columba, celebrations of Christ: 'Each saint is a manifestation of Christ; each bears the features of the Divine Model, but in a special and distinct manner.'[9] It is the Holy Spirit that refashions each of us into a living image of Christ, sharing his identity, but the work of the Spirit is like rain from heaven: though the same rain falls everywhere, it takes one form in the palm tree and another in the vine.[10] For Columba, to celebrate the feast's saints was to give glorify the work of Christ's grace in them. The Church admires and celebrates the saints, asking for God's help through their intercession. Turning to the saints in this way does not detract from Christ, but quite the opposite: Christ extends his action by giving us the graces for which we ask through them. 'Thus a supernatural current of exchange is established between all members of His mystical body.'[11] Columba saw that action of Christ is extended not diminished, when we receive graces in answer to their prayers.

At the heart of this vision is the gift of divine adoption, which is so fundamental to Columba's teaching. Because of our divine adoption, Christ shares all that is his with us: he shares his risen glory with the saints and they are one with him in all that he does for us; he shares his own prayer with the Church when it gathers for worship; he shares the mysteries of his life, death and resurrection with us in the feasts and seasons of the liturgical year.

    ℘   Christ being united to the Church gives her His power of adoring and praising God. The Church is united to Jesus and leans upon Him. Seeing her, the Angels ask: 'Who is this who cometh up from the desert, (but) flowing with delights, leaning on her Beloved?' It is the Church who, from the desert of her native poverty, mounts towards God, adorned like a virgin with the glorious treasures her Bridegroom gives her. And in the name of Christ, and with Him, she offers the adoration and praise of all her children to the Heavenly Father.[12]

    ℘   It is true that Christ Jesus is now glorious in heaven; His earthly life, in its physical duration and outward form, only lasted thirty-three years. But the virtue of each of these mysteries is infinite and remains inexhaustible. When we celebrate them in the holy liturgy, we receive from them, according to the measure of our faith, the same graces as if we had lived with Our Lord and been present at all His mysteries.[13]

෩

NOTES

1   The prayer 'Glory be to the Father, and to the Son, and to the Holy
     Spirit' that concludes each psalm in the daily prayer of the Church.

2   From his spiritual notes, Feast of the Blessed Trinity, 1888, cited in
     Raymund Thibaut, *Abbot Columba Marmion: A Master of the Spiritual
     Life 1858–1923* (London and Edinburgh: Sands & Co., 1932), p. 75.

3   CLS, p. 248.

4   CLS, p. 250.

5   CLS, p. 251. Here Columba is drawing on St Augustine.

6   CLS, p. 253.

7   CLS, p. 255.

8   CLS, p. 257.

9   CLS, p. 259.

10   This idea is from St Cyril of Jerusalem, *Catechesis* 16. I'm not sure if
     Columba was aware of this text, but his thought is similar.

11   CLS, p. 260.

12   CLS, p. 253.

13   CLS, p. 257.

CHAPTER SIXTEEN

Praying Through Christ Our Lord

ɛᴐ I felt today that we are pleasing to God in proportion as we are conformable to Jesus Christ, especially in His interior dispositions. This is why a *childlike* confidence in prayer, in spite of our sins is so pleasing to God. 'I know that Thou always hearest me,' said Jesus (to his Father). We are the adopted children of God and should always in all humility and simplicity treat Him in the same manner.[1]

The most important prayer for Blessed Columba was the prayer of the Church in the Mass and in the Divine Office. But personal prayer outside these liturgical celebrations held an important place for him too. 'A soul given to prayer profits more from the sacraments and other means of salvation than another whose prayer is without constancy and intensity,' he observes.[2] In teaching his fellow monks about prayer, he systematically considered methods of prayer, attitudes in prayer, progress in prayer and, above all the place of Christ in prayer. His teaching in this respect mostly concerns the kind of prayer where we address God freely rather than reciting prayers written by others. Both types of prayer are good.

Methods of prayer

As we have seen, Columba was well aware of the uniqueness of each person, and was at pains not to impose any one method of prayer for everyone. Each one has their own gift from Christ. After quoting a number of spiritual authorities on prayer, he said, 'To wish to impose indifferently on every soul one exclusive method would be not to take account the Divine liberty with which Christ Jesus distributes His grace, nor the attractions placed in us by the Holy Spirit.'[3] Among those he cited in support of this principle was the Jesuit founder St Ignatius Loyola, who wrote: 'For each one that meditation is the best in which God communicates Himself the most. For God knows and sees what is most suitable for us, and, knowing all, He Himself points out the way to be followed.'[4]

Columba did nonetheless make some broad suggestions. The first step, especially for beginners, was to reflect on some point of God's revelation to us. For example: if one were to reflect on the birth of Jesus, one might be begin to think about the humility of God, the poverty of the manger, the message of the angels, the joy of the Magi, and so on. This is because prayer is, for Columba, a conversation in which one both listens and speaks. To listen for the voice of God includes consideration of the ways in which God has revealed himself, especially in the life, death and resurrection of Jesus. Thoughtful reflection on the mysteries of our faith brings enlightenment, guidance, openness and sustenance to our intellect. It is the introduction to prayer, while prayer itself happens when the will is set on fire with love and enters into supernatural contact with God. Concretely, what happens is that at a certain point the person who is reflecting in this way spontaneously begins to speak to God in their own words about what they think and feel. Here reflection has moved to prayer itself, properly speaking. A specially inspired source for reflection and prayer, he explained, is the Bible.

Praying with the word of God

'The principal source of prayer is to be found in Holy Scripture read with devotion and reverence and laid up in the heart,' Columba maintained.[5] He placed particular emphasis on the Gospels and the letters of St Paul. In reading these, he said, we can contemplate the humanity of Christ, and this leads us to a knowledge of his divinity. Even though reflection or reading the scriptures involves a certain amount of mental effort on our part, Columba did not see prayer itself as the product of reasoning or purely natural effort; it is ultimately the work of the Holy Spirit in us. He wrote eloquently of the way in which the Holy Spirit can help us see just what we need to see in biblical passages:

> It is a flash of light that the Holy Spirit makes all at once to rise from the depth of the soul; it is like the sudden revelation of a source of life hitherto unsuspected, like a new and wider horizon that opens out before the soul; it is like a new world that the Spirit discovers to us.[6]

The process here flows naturally: attentive reading and reflection leads, under the inspiration of the Holy Spirit, to spontaneous prayer. This form of prayer was embedded in the monastic tradition to which Columba belonged and is sometimes called *lectio divina* (divine reading). One begins simply by reading the text, and then continues by 'chewing over' what is there. It is helpful to look out for things in the scripture passage that remind us of our life story; we can also notice any line that we find inspiring or uplifting; most importantly we look to see if it tells us anything about Christ. During this meditative process when we notice something significant we can pray to God in our own words, with great honesty and sincerity. This can sometimes lead to an intuitive sense that God is with us, that God has spoken to us, that God has heard our prayer. We can rest in that presence as long as the awareness lasts in a contemplative silence. When this is over we can go back to the text and read some more, setting off another cycle of reading, meditation, prayer and contemplation. What text should one choose for this form of meditative prayer? We can take a particular book of the Bible and read it from beginning to end, as Columba often did, but he also recommended taking the particular readings given in the Church's liturgical feasts and seasons as the inspiration for prayer. Some of his greatest inspirations came from meditating and praying in this way.

Attitudes in prayer

Our attitude as we pray was more important to Columba than the question of 'what to say'. Above all, he thought, it is 'our quality of children of God through the grace of Christ, that ought to determine our fundamental attitude in prayer.'[7] We come before God not just as creatures before the creator, but as sons and daughters in Jesus Christ. We can have the confidence to adopt towards God the same attitude as Jesus towards his heavenly Father, with simplicity and trust. When we pray it is Christ's gift of the Holy Spirit that prays within us (Rm 8:15).

Good communication involves turning towards the person with whom we speak, and turning away from other concerns. Prayer for Columba involved a deliberate turning to God. Most people get distracted in prayer, and his advice was that we simply turn back to God in a very gentle way as often as is necessary. He added that we should enter into prayer with a readiness to do God's will, whatever that might turn out to be. We should adopt a reverent attitude and a humble honesty about ourselves. Above all we are adopted sons and daughters of God just as Jesus is Son of God, and our prayer depends on him.

Depending on Christ

Columba said that we should lean on Christ in our prayer. We should unite ourselves to him and depend on him. We should have faith in his power to bring us to the Father. On this he quoted St Teresa of Ávila: 'God is extremely pleased to see a soul humbly place his Divine Son as the intermediary between it and Him.'[8] This is in fact what the Church does every time she prays 'through Christ our Lord'.

Developments in prayer

Columba spoke of the place of reasoning and reflection as an entry to prayer, especially for beginners. He added that, as prayer develops within a person, the process tends to simplify, with less reasoning, and the emergence of a more contemplative attitude. The reality of God is ultimately beyond anything our thoughts can grasp or words express. This means that a further development is a movement towards what he called 'prayer of quiet'. An image he used to describe this experience was an 'embrace of love'. He also pointed out that these are not watertight stages of development, and that God is free to give us different experiences of prayer that seem 'out of sequence'. One might add that it seems right to adopt the kind of prayer that appears most natural rather than trying to force a situation of 'quiet' or of 'contemplation' before God actually gives the gift. We don't have to try to force images and ideas out of our minds in order to attain quiet. A quiet sense of God's presence develops naturally when a more discursive approach simply falls away. Likewise one can leave reflection behind rather than trying to persist in it when God gives us something deeper. For example, when a person opens the scriptures in order to read and meditate on God's word, it can sometimes happen that a sense of God's presence arises straight away before they even look at the text, with a wordless prayer arising from the heart. This is not the moment to start reading, but to remain quietly turned towards God. When the contemplative moment passes, one can turn gently to reading again in order to launch prayer afresh. Columba also mentioned higher modes of operation where God's action in us is more profound again, sometimes producing ecstasy.

Columba noticed that joy is born within us as we pray. Whatever the style or 'method' we may use, 'that inward joy of being a child of God is made perfect little by little, and we have confidence it will reach its fullness one day in heavenly beatitude.'[9]

&ep; If we are united to Him by grace, Christ bears us with Him *Into the Holies* [Heb 9:12] as St Paul says, into 'the Holy of holies', the sanctuary of the divinity where, as Word, He is before all ages: *And the word was with God* [Jn 1:1].[10]

❧ The words of Christ ought to 'abide' in us so as to become in us principles of life; that is the reason too why it is useful for the soul that desires to live by prayer to read the Gospels constantly, and to follow the Church, our Mother, when she represents to us the actions and recalls the words of Jesus in the course of the liturgical cycle. In making all the stages of the life of Christ, her Bridegroom and our Elder Brother, pass before our eyes, the Church supplies us with abundant food for prayer.[11]

❧

NOTES

1   Columba's personal spiritual notes, Feast of the Sacred Heart, 1887, cited in Raymund Thibaut, *Abbot Columba Marmion: A Master of the Spiritual Life 1858–1923* (London and Edinburgh: Sands & Co., 1932), p. 61.

2   CLS, p. 262.

3   CLS, p. 268.

4   Letter of St Ignatius to St Francis Borgia, quoted in CLS, p. 267.

5   Letter dated 9 August 1920, cited in Raymund Thibaut, *Abbot Columba Marmion: A Master of the Spiritual Life 1858–1923* (London and Edinburgh: Sands & Co., 1932), p. 451.

6   CLS, p. 272.

7   CLS, p. 263.

8   Columba gives a simple footnote: Works vol. 1, p. 281.

9   CLS, p. 279.

10   CLS, p. 277.

11   CLS, p. 272.

CHAPTER SEVENTEEN

Our Neighbour is Christ

    Our Lord has made mutual charity His commandment and the object of his last prayer: *That they may BE PERFECT in one.* Let us strive to fulfil, as far as possible, this supreme wish of Christ's Heart. Love is a source of life, and if we draw forth this love from God so that it may be shed unfailingly upon all the members of the body of Christ, life will superabound within our souls, for Christ, according to His own promise, will pour down upon us, in return for our self-forgetfulness, a measure of grace 'good and pressed down, and shaken together and running over'.[1]

It might seem unusual that one has to wait until the seventeenth chapter of Blessed Columba's teaching before getting any detailed look at importance of loving our neighbour. This is because, for Columba, the first step was to love God in Christ, and love of neighbour flowed from this. He said:

    Let us then endeavour first of all to love God by keeping united to Our Lord: from this Divine love, as from a

glowing furnace whence a thousand rays shine forth
to give light and warmth, our charity will be extended
to all around us, and so much the further according as
the furnace is the more ardent. Our charity towards our
neighbour ought to radiate from our love of God.[2]

This explains his lengthy efforts to help us learn about loving God.
Love of neighbour was nonetheless essential for Columba. It was
said that he gave special preference to helping those who could
not repay his kindness, for example, his sister Rosie recounted that
one day as a young priest he was approached by a poor woman
looking for help. Having no money, he gave her his watch, which
was of considerable value. Later, as a teacher in Holy Cross
College, Dublin's seminary, he came to be well loved by the people
who lived in the surrounding district, and stories circulated about
the generous way he gave of his time and money to those who
were poor. Love of neighbour was important to Columba, and
his teaching hammered the point home with many quotes and
examples from the scriptures and the writings of the saints. He
began by pointing to the words of Jesus at the Last Supper as given
in the gospel according to John. Jesus prayed that we would all be
one, and gave a new commandment that we love one another. He
said that our love would be the sign to others that we were in fact
his disciples (Jn 13:15).

Our neighbour is Christ

Columba emphasised that every single human being is called to be
a member of the Body of Christ and that Christ has united himself
to all humanity. It follows then that love of the neighbour is love of
Christ. In the parable of the Last Judgement (Mt 25) Christ says,
'Whatever you did to the least of these who are members of my
family, you did it to me,' and commenting on this Columba said: 'To
abandon the least of our brethren is to abandon Christ Himself …
to touch one of the members of the body of Christ is to touch Christ
himself.'[3]

All of this, he pointed out, is entirely consistent with what he had already explained in talking about the Church and the sacraments. God has chosen to teach and lead us through mere human beings within the Church, and to make us holy through simple sacramental actions performed by others. Our union with Christ in the Eucharist is with the 'whole Christ', head and members. The measure in which we forgive others is the measure in which God forgives us. We cannot bypass others in our journey to God; this is not God's way. Columba said, 'Christ has become our neighbour, or rather our neighbour is Christ, presenting Himself to us under such or such a form.'[4] Underlining how we cannot pick and choose how Christ should present himself to us, he added: 'We only go to the Father by Christ; but we must accept Christ entirely, in Himself and in His members; there lies the secret of the true Divine life in within us.'

Saintly examples

We have already seen in how Columba drew attention to the example of the conversion of Saul (St Paul) to whom Jesus said, 'Why are you persecuting *me*?' Columba included other examples from the lives of saints to drive home how Christ can appear to us in the least likely forms. St Martin of Tours cut his cloak in half in order to share it with a beggar, only to see Christ himself wearing the same piece of cloth that night in a dream. Having no money to give to a poor man, St Catherine of Siena gave him a small silver cross, only for her to later have a vision in which she saw Christ holding the same cross, now encrusted with jewels, symbolising her love. St Teresa of Ávila pointed out that it is hard to know whether or not we really love God; the test is whether or not we love our neighbour.

Putting it into practice

Columba acknowledged that it is not always easy to love our neighbour. It needs a strong and generous love. Just as we need to persevere in prayer even when it seems dry and arid, so we need to persist in loving others even with the going gets tough. Great help can be found by looking at the gospels, seeing the way Jesus loved those around him and the generosity with which he responded to people in need. Particularly important is Jesus' forgiveness of others, for example: those who put him to death, the thief hanging on the cross beside him, the disciples who deserted him in his hour of crisis. Columba taught that praying for those who offend us was an important way of loving. No one deserves our hate, nor should they be excluded from our prayers.

We are called to love everyone, and with great generosity. But Columba pointed out that our love needs to be prudent and rightly ordered. For example, we have a particular duty towards our own blood relations: it would not normally be appropriate to give all our resources to those distant to us while neglecting family members who urgently need our help. I think of the commandment 'Honour your father and mother', which is about caring for elderly parents. Likewise, while it is a wonderful thing for parents to come to the help of those who are poorest and most at risk in society, they should not do this in such a way as to deprive their own children of what they need. Love will take a different tonality depending on our relationship with any particular person. For example, love for someone over whom we have been given responsibility and authority will be different to love for someone to whose authority we must answer.

All these things, according to Columba, spring from the same source: Christ, seen through faith, in our neighbour.

> ✍ I am sure that many souls will here find the reason of the difficulties, the sadness, the want of expansion in their inner life; they do not give themselves enough to Christ in the person of His members; they hold themselves back too much. If they would but give, it would be given to them and given abundantly; for Jesus Christ will not let Himself be outdone in love.[5]

> ✍ I do not fear to say that one who yields himself supernaturally and unreservedly to Christ in the person of his neighbour, loves Christ greatly and is infinitely loved

by Him; he will make great progress in union with Our Lord. While if you meet with one who devotes much time to prayer and, in spite of that, voluntarily shuts up his compassion against the necessities of his neighbour, you may hold it for certain that there is much illusion in his life of prayer.[6]

&

NOTES

1	CLS, p. 291.
2	CLS, p. 291.
3	CLS, p. 283.
4	CLS, p. 285.
5	CLS, p. 286.
6	CLS, p. 287.

CHAPTER EIGHTEEN

Our Mother in Christ

> ❧ We must be, like Jesus, *Filius Dei* and *Filius Mariae* [Son of God and Son of Mary]. He is both of these perfectly; if then we wish to produce His likeness within us, we must bear this two-fold quality.[1]

In his time at Holy Cross College, Clonliffe, Blessed Columba used to sign his name as Joseph A. Marmion, E. de M. (*Enfant de Marie*, Child of Mary). He prayed the rosary every day and chose the Sunday of the Rosary in October as the day for his blessing as Abbot. His teaching on Mary, then, and her important role in our lives was something especially precious to him. He considers her role as Mother of God, the special gifts given to her by God, and her close involvement in the redemptive work of Jesus, before considering possible aspects of devotion to her.

Jesus was born of a woman
Reflection on Mary, if it is to be good, begins and ends with Jesus. Columba begins with the identity of Jesus, both human and divine. In his divinity he is Son of God, but in his humanity he is Son of Mary. He owes his humanity to her. Columba mused that perhaps

God could have chosen to create a totally new human being from nothing, but he didn't. He chose to be born of a woman, and he chose Mary as his mother.

The motherhood of Mary was not imposed upon her. From the Gospel of the Annunciation (Lk 1:26-38) it is clear that her consent, freely given, was all-important. It was her 'yes' to God that made the conception of Jesus possible, and from that moment a world-changing event began. It is perhaps sobering to realise that so often we say 'no' when God's invitation to a more loving life is gently offered. Mary's consent to God's plan, despite the uncertainties and possible dangers it entailed, is sometimes referred to as her '*Fiat*', which is the Latin word for 'let it be done'. In the Gospel according to Saint Luke Mary says to the angel, 'Behold the servant of the Lord, *let it be done* to me according to your word.' Columba suggested that, as the journey of Jesus' life began to unfold, Mary would have had to renew her consent, her acceptance, her obedience to the will of God many times.

God's gifts to Mary

Columba outlines the very special gifts given by God to Mary in view of her extraordinary role in the incarnation of the Son of God: she was free from sin every moment of her life, and full of grace; she remained a virgin and, at the end of her earthly life, was assumed into heaven. A longer book could delve into the mysteries of these events and tease out what they might mean, but here we can only simply note that Columba mentioned these gifts without any significant elaboration. He suggested that we admire the gifts of God and give thanks for them. He proposed the Canticle of Mary – the *Magnificat*, as sung every day in the Church's Evening Prayer – as a model of such praise and thanksgiving.

Mary's cooperation with the work of Christ

While Mary is not mentioned often in the gospels, Columba pointed out that she does appear at pivotal moments in Christ's life. We have already mentioned his conception. At his birth, the shepherds in Bethlehem found Jesus with Mary and Joseph; the Magi, we are told, found him with his mother Mary. Together with Joseph she presented Jesus in the temple and also brought him there as a boy for the feast of Passover. She was present at Cana and was involved with the first sign of Jesus reported in the gospel according to John: the turning of water into wine. It was as a result of this that his disciples believed in him. Afterwards she went with him and his disciples to Capernaum. When she wasn't physically with Jesus she was still present to him, according to Columba, because she continued to ponder in her heart all that was said and done. In the Gospel according to John we also see her at the foot of the cross. Columba envisages her continuing to consent to God's mysterious plan even at this bleak moment. The beloved disciple is also there, and Jesus gives one to the other as mother and son. Biblical scholars believe that the Gospel according to John originated in an early Christian community that had close ties with the beloved disciple, and had received his testimony about Jesus. The beloved disciple is presented in this gospel as the ideal disciple, united to Jesus by love. This disciple, while being a real person, is proposed by the gospel according to John as model for each of us. Columba sees in this scene a special expression of Mary's maternity: in Christ, she is mother of every disciple. Like the beloved disciple, we are invited to take her into our home.

The basis of devotion to Mary

Columba based devotion to Mary, like so much else in his teaching, on our incorporation into Christ. We are all members of Christ's body; the good each person does benefits every member of the body. Of all his disciples, Mary is the closest to Christ. Columba quoted St Thomas Aquinas on this point: 'The nearer you come to a furnace, the more you feel the heat which radiates from it.'[2] Mary is inseparable from Christ and is thus intimately involved in all he does. She has a special maternal role in relation to the members of Christ's body.

The image of mothering as part of our life in Christ is not as strange as might first appear. Saint Paul in his letters used parental images to describe how he related to his first Gentile converts. He saw himself as a father and – while he may not come across as the most feminine of apostles – he also saw himself also as a mother, speaking of his own labour pains, struggling as his community came to birth in their new Christian identity (Gal 4:19).

We have already seen Jesus give Mary to the beloved disciple and to all of us. Columba also calls Mary the 'New Eve' while Christ is the 'New Adam'. This way of speaking may seem extravagant but it goes right back to the second century, and has roots in the scene at the foot of the cross in the Gospel of John. As he depicts it, the evangelist opens up a symbolic memory of the story of Adam and Eve. Eve was born from a rib in Adam's side, and the Church is born in the blood and water that flows from the side of Christ. Eve had been called 'woman' and 'mother of all who live', and Jesus addresses Mary as 'woman' as he gives her to the disciple as mother. She stands there at the birth of the Church as the new Eve. Columba does not elaborate any of these details, but his insistence on the motherhood of Mary in our lives is entirely biblical. If Saint Paul saw his parental role in terms of his preaching and teaching and praying, we might well ask: in what does the maternal role of Mary consist? A helpful answer is found, I believe in Pope Saint John Paul's encyclical on Mary, where he says that Mary exercises her maternal role by praying for us.[3]

The whole thrust of Columba's teaching as a whole is that we become by God's gift what Christ is by nature: human and divine. He pointed out that Jesus is Son of God and Son of Mary, and since he is our model, this should be true of us as well.

Drawing on such Church fathers as St Augustine and St Leo, Columba said that the second person of the Blessed Trinity was already spiritually present in Mary long before he was conceived physically in her womb: 'Mary first bore Jesus by faith and love, when, by her *Fiat*, she gave the awaited consent: *She conceived in her spirit before conceiving in her body.*' Going further, Columba says, 'Let us ask of her to obtain for us this faith that will make Jesus dwell in us: *That Christ may dwell by faith in your hearts;* this love which will make us live by the life of Jesus.'[4]

Expressing our devotion to Mary

Columba pointed firstly to the liturgy as the preeminent place where we express our devotion to Mary: in Marian feasts of the liturgical year and in the various prayers and hymns that are part of the liturgy from day to day. Outside the liturgy, he warned against overburdening ourselves with too many devotions, advising simply that we find something appropriate and remain faithful to it. Although he prayed the rosary every day, he didn't impose it as a necessary devotion for others but just proposed it as an admirable possibility. He thought that if we ask Mary every day to pray for us 'now and at the hour of our death' she would surely help us in a special way at the end of our earthly life. He also mentioned the 'Little Office of the Virgin Mary', the Litany of Our Lady and the Angelus as other possibilities. Concluding his presentation on Mary, he declared: 'The Virgin Mother has no greater wish than to see her Divine Son obeyed, loved, glorified and exalted.'[5]

    Those who do not know the Blessed Virgin, those who do not truly love the Mother of Jesus, run the risk of not profitably understanding the mysteries of Christ's Humanity. Christ is the Son of man as well as the Son of God; these two characters are essential to Him. If He is the Son of God by an eternal ineffable generation, He became Son of man by being born of Mary in time.[6]

    Now if Christ has become our Elder Brother in taking from Mary a nature like ours, which makes him one of our race, is it astonishing that, in dying, He should have given her to be our Mother in the order of grace who was His Mother according to human nature? ... In order to acknowledge the unique place Jesus has willed to give Mary in his mysteries and the love of the Blessed Virgin for us, we should give her the honour, love and confidence due to her as the Mother of Jesus and our Mother.[7]

৪৩

NOTES

1   CLS, p. 293.

2   *Summa Theologica*, III, q. XXVII, a. 5.

3   *Redemptoris Mater*, 40, https://www.vatican.va/content/john-paul-ii/en/encyclicals/documents/hf_jp-ii_enc_25031987_redemptoris-mater.html, accessed 22 September 2022.

4   CLS, p. 304.

5   CLS, p. 305.

6   CIHM, p. 419.

7   CLS, p. 299.

CHAPTER NINETEEN

Eternal Life in Christ

The glorification which awaits us and will be ours consists in this: We shall see God, we shall love God, we shall enjoy God. These acts constitute eternal life, the assured and full participation in the very life of God, and thence the beatitude of the soul, a beatitude in which the body is to share after the resurrection.[1]

When Blessed Columba was on his deathbed, one of his monks asked him, 'Father Abbot, are you happy to go to heaven?' He replied, 'The Will of God.' On other occasions he answered the same question saying, 'Very happy, yes, very happy.' It seems fitting then to end by looking at his teaching on the joy of heaven, given in his final talk in the series later published as *Christ, the Life of the Soul*.

Our hope of eternal life in Christ
The recurring theme of Columba's teaching is that we are, by God's gift, sons and daughters of God, sharing in the dignity of Christ himself, the Son of God. Columba pointed to an important implication, found in St Paul: if we share in this grace of adoption, then we are also joint heirs with Christ (Rm 8:17). 'The same

inheritance which is Christ's is to become ours – eternal life, glory and beatitude in the inheritance of God.'[2] This is the full flowering of the life of Christ in us, a gift that was given to us in baptism.

> ∞ The life of Christ in us here below by grace is like the dawn of day; it only attains its noon-tide – a noon-tide without decline – if it comes to its fullness in glory. Baptism is the source whence the Divine river rises; but this river, which makes glad the city of souls, flows at last into the ocean of eternity. That is why we shall only have an incomplete idea of the life of Christ in our souls if we do not contemplate the end which, of its nature, it must reach.[3]

Columba said that we should think about this promise of eternal life often.

The happiness of heaven

Columba taught that our likeness to Christ will be complete in heaven. We shall be like Christ (1 Jn 3:2). Because of the life of Christ within us, we will love God with a love that is powerful and pure, perfect and eternal. The instability of our love while on earth will be over. Furthermore, we will *enjoy* God. Columba saw in the Book of Psalms a prophecy of this joy: the elect 'shall be inebriated with the plenty of thy house: and Thou shall make them drink of the torrent of Thy pleasures. For with Thee is the fountain of life' (Ps 35:9). God's own joy will be ours: 'enter into the joy of your Lord' (Mt 25:21). Death shall be no more.

Columba reminds us that even our bodies, raised up and transformed, will share in the joy of heaven, and we will be part of a multitude too large to be counted, praising God for his kindness and his mercy. The more we have grown in love on earth, the greater will be our joy in heaven. Because of this, he wrote, we should 'yield ourselves to Christ with every energy of body and soul, to seek, like Him, to do always, through love, what pleases our Heavenly Father'.[4] It is entirely fitting then that his concluding words in *Christ, the Life of the Soul* are addressed to Christ himself, in a prayer that sums up so much of what he had to say.

The spirituality of this prayer is based on the incarnation of the Son of God, who became one of us so that we might share, with him, in the life of God. Insofar as we are holy, it is a sharing in the holiness of Christ, a sharing indeed in the Holy Spirit, so that we live by his power and goodness and so that the mysteries of his life, death and resurrection are replicated in us. The work of the Holy Spirit overcomes all that is opposed to our sharing in the life of the Holy Trinity itself. This prayer expresses the theology of St Paul, so dear to Columba: 'It is no longer I who lives, but Christ who lives in me' (Gal 2:20). Through Christ, with Christ, and in Christ we have the power to become fully human and fully divine, to the glory of God the Father. This is Columba's message, and it remains a source of light and encouragement today. Without this doctrine of our divine adoption, Christianity is in danger of shrinking into a moralistic series of do's and don'ts that inspires nobody. With it, our faith becomes confident, buoyant and free with the liberty of the children of God.

ℬ O Christ Jesus, Incarnate Word, Son of Mary,
   come and live in Thy servants with Thy Spirit of holiness,
   the fullness of Thy power,
   the reality of Thy virtues,
   the perfection of Thy ways,
   the communication of Thy mysteries,
   and overcome all hostile powers by Thy Spirit
   to the glory of the Father. Amen.[5]

ℬ

NOTES

1	CLS, p. 308.
2	CLS, p. 307.
3	CLS, p. 307.
4	CLS, p. 316.
5	CLS, p. 316.